Édouard Duquet

A New and Easy Method of Instruction in Pronouncing and Speaking the French Language

Containing a selcetion of words and phrases most in use in familiar conversations

Édouard Duquet

A New and Easy Method of Instruction in Pronouncing and Speaking the French Language

Containing a selcetion of words and phrases most in use in familiar conversations

ISBN/EAN: 9783337393083

Printed in Europe, USA, Canada, Australia, Japan

Cover: Foto ©Andreas Hilbeck / pixelio.de

More available books at **www.hansebooks.com**

A NEW AND EASY METHOD

OF INSTRUCTION IN

PRONOUNCING AND SPEAKING

THE

FRENCH LANGUAGE,

CONTAINING A SELECTION OF

WORDS AND PHRASES MOST IN USE

IN FAMILIAR CONVERSATIONS.

BY

EDOUARD DUQUET,

PROFESSOR OF FRENCH IN THE DRURY ACADEMY AND GRADED AND HIGH SCHOOL OF

ADAMS, MASS.

NORTH ADAMS, MASS.:
ANGELL & MANDEVILLE, PRINTERS.
1870.

Entered, according to Act of Congress, in the year 1870, by
EDOUARD DUQUET,
In the Office of the Librarian of Congress, at Washington.

PREFACE.

The object of the present work is to impart to the student of the French Language, in a short time, and in the easiest possible way, a correct pronunciation, void of the slightest English accent, with the help of a native French teacher, or even by self-instruction.

The characteristic feature of my system is to enable the learner to master, with thoroughness, the standard sounds of the French Language; special attention being paid to the nasal and liquid sounds, without a correct pronunciation of which the student might as well undertake a trip to the Moon, as to try to make his French understood to those speaking the French Language.

This method is divided into three parts; the first two being subdivided into short lessons.

The first part gives the sound of each letter of the alphabet when alone, and also in the different combinations in which it occurs.

The second part, which is probably the most important of the method, is devoted to the spelling of words in French, exercises on the nasal and liquid sounds, explanation on the connexion of words and on pauses in reading, and ending with reading lessons in prose and poetry, translated into English, so that the student by understanding what he reads can give the emphasis.

In the third part are the two verbs *avoir* and *être* conjugated affirmatively, negatively and interrogatively, with different nouns to show their position in the sentence. There is also a selection of words and phrases commonly used in speaking French, thus enabling the student, after a careful study of the method, not only to pronounce correctly, but also rendering him capable of conversing on familiar topics.

EDOUARD DUQUET.

DRURY ACADEMY, North Adams, Mass., *November* 1, 1870.

DUQUET'S METHOD OF INSTRUCTION

IN PRONOUNCING AND SPEAKING THE

FRENCH LANGUAGE.

PART FIRST.

LESSON I.

ALPHABET.

A   B   C   D   E   F   G   H   I   J   K
ah. bay. say. day. uh. ef. zhay. ash. e. zhe. kah.

L   M   N   O   P   Q   R   S   T   U
el. m. n. o. pay. ku. air. ess. tay. nearly like *ee* in *her*.

V   X   Y   Z
vay. eeks. egrec. zed.

Vowels.

A   E   I   O   U   Y

Consonants.

B C D F G H J K L M N P Q R S T V X Z

THE VOWELS.

Lesson II.

Vowels take a longer or shorter sound when accented. There are three sorts of accents.
1. The *acute* accent (´) which is placed only over é to give it the sound of an English *a*.
2. The grave accent (`) is placed over è, giving to that vowel an open sound, as *e* in met. It is also put on à, *at* or *to*, là, there; dejà, already; and on the ù of où, where; but does not change the sound of these letters.
3. The *circumflex* accent (ˆ) is placed over â ê î ô û, and gives to those vowels a longer sound.

A.

A is pronounced like *a* in *cat*. Example: préface, *preface ;* salle, *hall ;* table, *table ;* â like *a* in *far ;* Ex. âme, *soul;* bâtir, *to build;* mât, *mast*.

E.

E like *uh*. Ex. me, *me;* te, *thee;* que, *that*. *e* final is generally silent in polysyllables. Ex. table, *table;* peuple, *people*. é, like *a* in *gate*. Ex. été, *summer;* élevé, *raised*. è like *e* in *met*. Ex. frère, *brother;* lève, *raise;* espère, *hope;* ê like *a*, in *care*. Ex. même, *same;* carême, *lent;* bête, *beast*.

Lesson III.

I.

I, like *ee* in *see*. Ex. lit, *bed;* dit, *said;* ici, *here*. î, like *ee*, in *feel*. Ex. île, *isle;* gîte, *lodging;* dîme, *tithe*.

O.

O, like *o* in *no*. Ex. m*o*t, *word;* rep*o*s, *rest;* tr*o*t, *trot*. *ô* like *o* in *bone*. Ex. dép*ô*t, *deposit;* t*ô*t, *soon;* prév*ô*t, *provost*.

U.

U, nearly like *e* in *her*. Ex. b*u*, *drank;* d*u*, *of the;* l*u*ne, *moon*. *û* is *u* with a longer sound. Ex. m*û*r, *ripe;* ch*û*te, *fall;* d*û*, *due*.

Y.

Y, initial, between two vowels, or forming a syllable by itself, is pronounced like the French *i*, or *ee* in *reed*. Ex. *y*, *there;* t*y*pe, *type;* *y*eux, *eyes*. *y* between two vowels has the power of two *i*'s. Ex. mo*y*en, *means;* pa*y*er, *to pay*. These words are pronounced *moi-ien, pai-ier*.

THE DIPHTHONGS AND COMBINED VOWELS.

Lesson IV.

A vowel with a diaeresis (¨) over it is pronounced separately; it cannot form a diphthong with the preceding or the following vowel. Ex. maïs, *indian-wheat*. There are, however, a few words in which the ë final is silent, as in ciguë, pronounced sig*û*. *E* accented (é), and preceding a vowel, is pronounced separately. Ex. obéir, *to obey;* géant, *giant*.

ai, ei.

Ai, ei, preceding a liquid *l,* do not form a diphthong; a*i*l, a*i*lle, are pronounced like the word *eye;* and e*i*l, e*i*lle, like *āye.* (See Liquid Sounds.) Ex. port*ai*l, *portal;* can*ai*lle, *rabble;* par*ei*l, *alike;* abe*i*lle, *bee.* *Ai,* followed by a final, *s, t* or *d,* takes a broad sound resembling the French *è,* or *e* in *met.* Ex. je dis*ai*s, *I said ;* il dis*ai*t, *he said ;* l*ai*d, *ugly.* The diphthong *ai* is pronounced everywhere else like a French *é,* or *a* in *fate.* Ex. j'*ai, I have;* j'ir*ai, I will go.*

au.

Au, not as broad as *ah!* in English, and *eau* are pronounced alike. Ex. ch*au*d, *warm;* b*eau, handsome;* chap*eau, hat.*

Lesson V.

ei.

Ei, like *a* in *gate.* Ex. n*ei*ge, *snow;* s*ei*ne, *seine;* r*ei*ne, *queen.*

eu.

Eu, like *e* in *her.* Ex. p*eu, little;* l*eu*r, *their;* chal*eu*r, *heat.* *eu,* of the verb *avoir, to have;* j'*eu*s, *I had,* is pronounced like a simple *u.*

ia.

Ia, like *ia,* in *cordial.* Ex. il n*ia, he denied;* il pr*ia, he prayed;* d*ia*metre, *diameter.*

ie.

Ie, like *ee* in *bee*. Ex. il n*ie*, *he denies;* garant*ie*, *guarantee;* harp*ie*, *harpy*.

oi.

Oi, like *wa* in *war*. Ex. b*oi*s, *wood;* v*oi*x, *voice;* r*oi*, *king;* dr*oi*t, *right*.

ou.

Ou, like *oo* in *fool*. Ex. n*ou*s, *we;* b*ou*t, *end;* d*ou*x, *soft;* l*ou*p, *wolf*.

ua, ue, ui, uo.

Ua, ue, ui, uo, have no corresponding sound in English; *ua*, n*ua*ge, *cloud; ue*, like *u* alone, n*ue*, *cloud; ui*, l*ui*, *him; uo*, d*uo*, *duet*.

THE CONSONANTS.

Lesson VI.

Most initial consonants are sounded as in English. Final consonants are generally silent; *c, f, l, r,* final, are generally pronounced. The final consonant is generally carried to the next word when that word begins with a vowel or an *h* mute.

B.

B initial is pronounced as in English. In the middle of words, and at the end of proper nouns, *b* is sounded. Ex. a*b*strait, *abstract;* Jaco*b*, *Jacob*.

b is silent in plom*b*, *lead;* surplom*b*, *slope;* d'aplom*b*, *level;* tireplom*b*, *glacier's vice.* When two *b*'s come in contact, only one of these letters is pronounced. Ex. a*bb*aye, *abbey.*

C.

C has the sound of *k* before *a, o, u, l, n, r.* Ex. *c*acher, *to conceal;* *c*ou, *neck;* dé*c*uple, *decuple;* dé*c*lin, *decline;* *c*néius, *cneius;* *c*roix, *cross.* *C* preceding *e* and *i*, and with the cedilla (*ç*) before *a, o, u*, has the sound of *s.* Ex. *c*eci, *this;* fa*ç*ade, *front;* le*ç*on, *lesson;* re*ç*u, *received.* *Ch* has the sound of *sh* in *she.* Ex. *ch*anger, *to exchange.* *Ch* is pronounced like *k* in *ch*os, *ch*ronique, or*ch*estre, patriar*ch*at, ana*ch*ronisme, Mi*ch*el-Ange, *ch*oeur, in all words having *chre, chri, chro, chry,* and in words derived from the Greek language. It is elsewhere generally pronounced as *sh.* *C* preceded by *n* is not sounded. Ex. ban*c, bench.* It is also silent in taba*c, snuff;* estoma*c, stomach;* cler*c, clerk;* la*cs, noose;* mar*c, grounds;* éche*cs, checks;* por*c, hog;* bro*c, pitcher;* *c* is sounded elsewhere. *C* final is not generally carried to the next word; it is sounded as *g* in second and in derivations.

Lesson VII.

D.

D is pronounced as in English. Ex. *d*iner, *to dine.* The final *d* is silent except in proper names. Ex. *David.* *D* final takes the sound of *t* before a vowel or an *h* mute. Ex. gran*d*-arbre, gran*d*-homme, pronounced *grān-tarbre, grān-tomme*.

Lesson VIII.

F.

F is pronounced as in English. Ex. *f*igure, *figure*. The final *f* is sounded, except in the following words: cle*f*, *key;* cer*f*, *stag;* éteu*f*, *tennis ball;* ner*f*s, *nerves;* bœu*f*s, *oxen;* œu*f*s, *eggs;* œu*f* frais, *fresh egg;* œu*f* dur, *hard egg;* bœu*f* salé, *salt beef;* che*f*-d'œuvre, *masterpiece;* cer*f*-volant, *kite*. The *f* of neu*f*, *nine*, is sounded like *v* before a word commencing with a vowel or an *h* mute.

G.

G is not sounded in san*g*, *blood;* étan*g*, *pond;* ran*g*, *rank;* haren*g*, *herring;* sein*g*, *signature;* poin*g*, *fist;* vin*g*t, *twenty;* doi*g*t, *finger;* faubour*g*, *suburb;* le*g*s, *legacy;* and in proper names, as Strasbour*g*, Edinbour*g*. *G* final is sounded like *k* before a vowel or an *h* mute. Ex. ran*g* honorable is pronounced *rān-konorable*. *G* is always sounded hard (like *g* in *garrison*) before *a*, *o*, *u*. Ex. *g*ant, *glove;* *g*orge, *throat;* ai*g*u, *acute*. *G*, preceding *e*, *i*, is always soft (like *su* in *measure*). Ex. *g*elée, *frost;* *g*îte, *lodging*. *G*ua, *g*uo, *g*ue, *g*ui are pronounced *g*ha, *g*ho, *g*he, *g*hi. Ex. il lé*g*ua, *he bequeathed;* *g*uerre, *war*. The two vowels *ui* are, however, sounded in ai*g*u*i*lle, *needle*. *U*e of *g*ue final is silent except when there is a diæresis over the *ë*. Ex. *ue* silent; or-*gue*, organ; *ue* sounded, cig*uë*, hemlock; *gn*. (See liquid Sounds.)

Lesson IX.
H.

Over fifteen hundred words in French have *h* initial, four hundred of which are aspirated, and the rest have *h* mute. *H* mute has no sound by itself, and is treated as a vowel when following a word subject to elision; as bon*s h*ommes, *good men;* pronounced *bōn zommes*. *H* aspirate is always initial, and is slightly accented. *H* is sometimes final, but never double. The final consonant of a word is never connected with the following word if that word commences with an *h* aspirate. The following are some of the words generally used having *h* aspirate:

Hableur,	Halle,	Haras,
Hache,	Hallebarde,	Harasser,
Hagard,	Hallier,	Harceler,
Haie,	Halte,	Hardes,
Haillons,	Hamac,	Hardi,
Haine,	Hameau,	Harem,
Hair,	Hanche,	Hareng,
Haire,	Hangar,	Hargneux,
Hâler,	Hanneton,	Haricot,
Halage,	Hanter,	Haridelle,
Hâle,	Harangue,	Harnais,

Harpe,	Hérisser,	Houblon,
Harpie,	Heron,	Houille,
Harpon,	Heros,	Houlette,
Hasard,	Hêtre,	Houppe,
Hâter,	Herse,	Houri,
Hausser,	Heurter,	Houpp,
Haut,	Hibon,	Housse,
Hautbois,	Hideux,	Houx,
Hautesse,	Hiérarchie,	Huche,
Have,	Hoguet,	Huée,
Havre,	Hollande,	Huguenot,
Havresac,	Homard,	Huit,
Héler,	Houte,	Humer,
Hennir,	Horde,	Huppe,
Henri,	Hors,	Hure,
Hérant,	Hottentot,	Hurler,
Hérisson,	Hotte,	Hussard.

LESSON X.

J.

J is pronounced like *s* in measure. Ex. *j*amais, *never; j*ardin, *garden; j*our, *day; j*uste, *just*.

K.

K is sounded like *k* in English. Ex. *k*ali, *kali; k*an, *khan; k*épi, *military cap; k*ilogramme, a *French weight*.

L.

L final, coming after *a, e, o, u,* is generally sounded. Ex. ba*l*, *ball;* se*l*, *salt;* so*l*, *soil;* seu*l*, *alone.* L single or *l* double, preceded by the vowel *i*, generally takes a liquid sound. Ex. porta*il, portal;* fi*lle, daughter;* etc., etc. (See Liquid Sounds.)

M, N.

M and *N*, preceded by a vowel, ending a syllable, or immediately followed by a consonant, are sounded nasal. (See Nasal Sounds.) Final consonants following *m* or *n* are not sounded. Ex. ven*t, wind;* tem*ps, weather.* *N* final, except in no*n,* is carried over to the next word if it commences with a vowel or *h* mute, if these two words are closely connected, as in so*n* argent, *his silver;* bo*n* ami, *good friend;* pronounce *son nargent, bon nami.* (See Connexion of Words.) *M* is silent in da*m*nable, *damnable;* da*m*nablement, *damnably;* da*m*nation, *damnation;* da*m*ner, *to damn;* conda*m*ner, *to condemn;* auto*m*ne, *autumn.*

Lesson XI.
P.

P undergoes no change except when followed by the consonant *h;* both consonants are then sounded like *f*. Ex. *p*hilosophe, *philosopher;* pronounced *fee-lo-zof.* *P* is generally sounded as in English. It is, however, not articulated in ba*p*tiser, *to baptize;* ba*p*tême, *baptism;* com*p*te, *account;* dom*p*ter, *to subdue;* exem*p*t, *exempt;* se*p*t, *seven;* se*p*tième, *seventh.* *P* final is silent. Ex. cham*p, field;* cam*p, camp;* cou*p, blow;* dra*p, cloth.* It is sounded in ca*p*, *cape*; and in most proper names. The final *p* is not carried to the following word.

Q.

Q final must never be sounded in cin*q*, *five*, when followed by a word commencing with a consonant. Ex. cin*q* tables, *five tables*. *Q* is also silent in co*q*-d'inde, *turkey-cock*. Elsewhere it is sounded. *Qu* has the sound of *k*. Ex. *qu*and, *when;* *qu*e, *that;* *qu*i, *who;* *qu*oi, *what;* *qu*estion, *question*. *Ue* final coming after *q* is silent. Ex. bouti*que*, *shop*. *Qu* is pronounced as in English in the words, é*qu*ation, a*qu*atique, é*qu*ateur, *qu*adruple, *qu*adrupède, *qu*adrangulaire, in-*qu*arto, é*qu*estre, é*qu*itation, li*qu*ifier, *qu*intelurce, *qu*intilier, *qu*intuple, *qu*irinal.

Lesson XII.

R.

The French *r* is pronounced with more force than the English. *rr* is pronounced like a single *r*. Ex. a*rr*anger, *to arrange*, is pronounced *a-ranger*. Both *r*'s are, however, distinctly sounded in the future and conditional of acquérir, *to acquire;* courir, *to run;* and mourir, *to die*. Ex. j'acque*rr*ai, je cou*rr*ais. The two *r*'s are also sounded in te*rr*eur, *terror;* ho*rr*eur, *horror;* e*rr*er, *to wonder;* abe*rr*ation, *aberration;* abho*rr*er, *to abhor;* e*rr*ata, *errata;* na*rr*er, *to relate;* and in words commencing with *irr*. Ex. i*rr*uption, *irruption*. *R* final is always sounded when preceded by *a, i, o, u;* but it is generally silent when preceded by the vowel *e,* the combined letters *er* having the sound of an English *a* or French *é.* Ex. dang*er, danger,* is pronounced *dangé.* *R* is sounded in am*er,* ch*er,* belved*er,* enf*er,* canc*er,* cuill*er,* f*er,* eth*er,* fi*er,* hi*er,* hiv*er,* frat*er,* lucif*er,* mâchef*er,* m*er,* outre-m*er.*

Lesson XIII.

S.

S medial is sounded like *z,* or as in the English word *rose* when placed between two vowels. Ex. cho*s*e, *thing.* It preserves its natural sound when initial, and in the following words: para*s*ol, *parasol;* vrai*s*emblance, *probability;* monosyllabæ, *monosyllables;* and derivations; also in co*s*aque, a*s*ymbole, dé*s*uétude, tourne*s*ol, pré*s*éance, pre*s*upposer, gi*s*ant, nous gi*s*ons. The final *s* is always silent in the plural of substantives, and in any word whatever, except in the connexion of words, and in the following words: atla*s, atlas;* aloe*s, aloes;* a*s, ace;* héla*s, alas;* lap*s, lapse;* florè*s, flourish;* bi*s, once more;* grati*s, gratis;* blocu*s, blockade;* choru*s, chorus;* cen*s, census;* en su*s, besides;* lapi*s, lapis;* iri*s, iris;* our*s, bear;* hiatu*s, gaps;* phébu*s, phœbus;* prospectu*s, prospectus;* vi*s, screw;* orému*s, oremus.* *S* is pronounced in fil*s, son;* and in tou*s* when taken substantively. *S* is also sounded in Chri*s*t, but not in Jé*s*us-Christ; pronounced *Kreest* and *Jesu-Kree.*

S is carried to the next word when that word commences with a vowel or an *h* mute, and it takes then the sound of *z*. Ex. bons enfants, *good children;* bons habits, *good coats;* pronounced *bon zenfants, bon zabits.*

Lesson XIV.

T.

T, immediately followed by *ial, iel, ion*, has the sound of *c* in most of French words which are spelled alike and have the same meaning in English, and in which *ti* is pronounced *she*. Ex. mar*t*ial, *martial;* essen*t*iel, *essential;* por*t*ion, *portion*. *T* has also the sound of *c* in words ending in *atie* and having in English the termination *cy*. Ex. democra*t*ie, *democracy*. Pronounce *t* like *c* in pa*t*ience, *patience;* ini*t*er, *to initiate;* minu*t*ie, *minutia;* Dalma*t*ie, *Dalmatia;* Egyp*t*ien, *Egyptian;* inep*t*ie, *absurdity;* Dalma*t*ien, *Dalmatian.* But in most other words ending in *tie, tié, tier, t* preserves its natural sound. Ex. garantie, *gurantee;* moitié, *half;* portier, *porter.* *T*, followed by *ions* or *iez*, in verbs, or preceded by *x* or *s*, has its proper sound. Ex. nous ê*t*ions, *we were;* vous êtiez, *you were;* ques*t*ion, *question;* mix*t*ion, *mixtion*. The final *t* is always silent, except in the connexion of words, and in the following words: exac*t*, *exact;* fa*t*, *coxcomb;* opia*t*, *opiate;* cobal*t*, *cobalt;* rap*t*, *rape;* yach*t*, *yacht;* es*t*, *east;* oues*t*, *west;* lice*t*, *permission;* les*t*, *ballast;* zes*t*, *fiddlestick;*

2*

direc*t*, *direct;* tace*t*, *secret;* e*t* cetera, *and so on;* iufec*t*, *infect;* accessi*t*, *near it;* grani*t*, *granite;* sep*t*, *seven;* hui*t*, *eight* (the *t* of these last- two words is sounded except when followed by a word commencing with a consonant); défici*t*, *deficiency;* subi*t*, *sudden;* taci*t*, *silent;* stric*t*, *strict;* prétéri*t*, *preterite;* transit, *permit;* Chris*t* (*t* is not sounded in Jésus-Chris*t*); zeni*th*, *zenith* (*th*, initial, medial or final, is always sounded like *t*); do*t*, *dowry;* bru*t*, *rough;* lu*th*, *lute;* chu*t*, *hush;* indul*t*, *favor*. *T* is carried to the next word when the two words are closely connected, as ce*t* ami, *that friend;* pronounced *cé tami*. The *t* of the conjunction e*t* (and) is never carried to the next word, and is always silent.

Lesson XV.

V, W.

V single and *v* double (*w*) are pronounced alike; the latter is only used in foreign words. Ex. *W*urtemberg, pronounced *V*ertembourg. *W* is pronounced as in English in *whist* and whig.

X.

X, initial, or placed between *e* initial and a vowel or an *h* mute, is pronounced like *gz*. Ex. *X*énophon, *Xenophon;* e*x*iler, *to exile;* e*x*hiber, *to exhibit*. *X*, between two vowels, but not following the initial *e*, has the sound of *ks*. Ex. se*x*e, *sex;* lu*x*e, *luxury*. *X* has the sound of *ss* in si*x*, *six;* di*x*, *ten;* soi*x*ante, *sixty;* Bru*x*elles, *Brussels;* Au*x*onne, Ai*x*-en-Provence, Au*x*erne. In si*x*ième, di*x*ième, deu*x*ième, di*x*-huit, di*x*-huitième, di*x*-neuf, di*x*-neuvième, *x* is pronounced like *z*. The final *x* is generally silent; it is never sounded in the plural of any word, except in the connexion of words where it is pronounced like *z*. Ex. voi*x* enrouée, *hoarse voice;* pronounced *voi zenrouée.* *X* is sounded (*ks*) in the following words: clima*x*, *climax;* pheni*x*, *phœnix;* inde*x*, *index;* sphin*x*, *sphinx;* aja*x*, Sty*x*, and in ai*x*-lachapellé. The *x* of deu*x*, si*x*, di*x*, is silent when before a word commencing with a consonant. Ex. si*x* livres, *six books*, is pronounced *see livrr.*

Z.

The final *z* is never sounded except in connexion of words, in ga*z*, *gas,* and in a few proper names, as Suez, Metz, Alvarez, etc. Carry the final *z* to the next word when that word commences with a vowel or an *h* mute.

END OF PART FIRST.

PART SECOND.

SPELLING LESSONS.

Lesson I.

Accents and Signs.

French.	Pronunciation.	Translation.
Accent aigu,	(´) AK-SĀN-TAY-GÜ,	acute accent.
accent grave,	(`) AK-SĀN-GRĀV,	open accent.
accent circonflex,	(^) AK-SĀN-SEER-ĒON FLEX,	circumflex accent.
tréma,	(¨) TRAY-MAH,	diæresis.
cédille,	(ç) SAY-DEEL,	cedilla.
apostrophe,	(') AH-POSST-ROF,	apostrophe.

Spelling of accented letters.

French.	Sound of accented vowels.	Sound of not acc'd vowels.	Pronunciation.	Sound of accented vowels.
â, accent circonflex,	AHH,	AH,	AK-SĀN-SEER-KŌN-FLEX,	AHH.
é, accent aigu,	A,	UH,	AK-SĀN-TAY-GÜ,	A.
è, accent grave,	AI,	UH,	AK SĀN-GRR-HAV,	AI.
ê, accent circonflex,	AY,	UH,	AK-SĀN-SEER-KŌN-FLEX,	AY.
î, accent circonflex,	EE,	E,	AK-SĀN SEER-KŌN-FLEX,	EE.
ô, accent circonflex,	Ō,	O,	AK-SĀN-SEER-KŌN-FLEX,	Ō.
û, accent circonflex,	Ū,	U,	AK-SĀN-SEER-KŌN-FLEX,	Ū.

Lesson II.

Spelling of words with accented letters.

French.	Pronunciation.	
â-me,	AHH-M,	â, accent circonflex, â, AHH; m-e, MUH; â-me, AHH-M; soul.
blâ-me,	BLAHH-M,	b-l-â, accent circonflex, blâ, BLAH; m-e, MUH; blâ-me, BLAHH-M; blame.
é-té,	A-TAY,	é, accent aigu, é, A; t-é, accent aigu, té, TAY; é-té, A-TAY; summer.
é-le-vé,	A-LUH-VAY,	é, accent aigu, é, A; l-e, LUH; é-le, A-LUH; v-é, accent aigu, vé, VAY; é-le-vé, A-LUH-VAY; raised.
mê-me,	MAY-M,	m-ê, accent circonflex, mê, MAY; me, MUH; mê-me, MAY-M; same.
cra-tè-re,	KRAH-TAI-RR,	c-r-a, cra, KRAH; t-è, accent grave, tè, TAI; cra-tè, KRAH-TAI; re, RUH; cra-tè-re, KRA-TAI-RR.
dî-ner,	DEE-NAY,	d-î, accent circonflex, dî, DEE; n-e-r, ner, NAY; dî-ner, DEE-NAY; to dine.
dé-pôt,	DAY-PŌ,	d-é, accent aigu, dé, DAY; p-ô, accent circonflex, t, pôt, PŌ; dé-pôt, DAY-PŌ; depot.

French.	Pronunciation.	
fú-mes,	FŪ-M,	*f-ú,* accent circonflex, *fú,* FŪ ; *m-e-s, mes,* MUH ; *fú-mes,* FŪH-M ; were.
ma-ïs,	MAH-ISS,	*m-a, ma,* MAH ; *ï,* tréma, *s, ïs,* ISS; *ma-ïs,* MAH-ISS; maize.

LESSON III.

Spelling of words with apostrophe and cedilla.

de, ce, le, la, me, ne, se, que.
d', c', l', l', m', n', s', qu'.

When any of the above words are placed before a word commencing with a vowel or an *h* mute, its vowel *e* or *a* is taken away, and the two words are united by an apostrophe (').

C with a cedilla under it (*ç*) is sounded like *s.* (See *C.*)

French.	Pronunciation.	
d'or	DOR,	*d',* apostrophe, *or, d'or,* DOR, of gold.
c'é-tait,	SAY-TAI,	*c',* apostrophe, *é,* accent aigu, *c'é,* SAY ; *t-a-i-t, tait,* TAI ; *c'é-tait,* SAY-TAI ; it was.
l'au-tre,	LO-TRE,	*l',* apostrophe, *au, l'au,* LO ; *t-r-e, tre,* TRUH ; *l'au-tre,* LO-TRR ; the other.
il m'ai-me,	EEL-MAY-M,	*il,* EEL ; *m',* apostrophe, *ai, m'ai,* MAY ; *me,* MUH ; *il m'ai-me,* EEL MAY-M ; he loves me.

DUQUET'S METHOD. 23

French.	Pronunciation.	
n'est,	NAI,	n', apostrophe, est, n'est, NAI, is not.
s'ai-der,	SAY-DAY,	s', apostrophe, ai, s'ai, SAY; der, DAY; s'ai-der, SAY-DAY; to help one's self.
qu'il,	KEEL,	qu', apostrophe, il, qu'il, KEEL, that he.
le-çon,	LUH-SŎN,	le, LUH; ç, cédille, on, çon, SŎN; le-çon, LUH-SŎN; lesson.

LESSON IV.
Exercise.

French.	Pronunciation.	Translation.
Al-ler,	AH-LAY,	to go.
Bâ-tir,	BAHH-TEER,	to build.
Ca-va-le-rie,	KAH-VAH-LREE,	cavalry.
Dé-ter-mi-ner,	DAY-TAIR-MEE-NAY,	to determine.
É-cla-bous-ser,	A-KLAH-BOOS-SAY,	to splash.
Fla-bel-li-for-me,	FLAH-BAI-LEE-FORM,	fan-shaped.
Go-ni-o-mè-tre,	GO-NEE-O-MAI-TRR,	gonometer.
Ha-bi-le-té,	AH-BEE-LUH-TAY,	skill.
I-ma-gi-na-tif,	E-MAH-ZHEE-NAH-TIF,	imagination.
Ja-co-bi-nis-me,	ZHAH-KO-BEE-NEES-M,	Jacobinism.
Ki-lo-gram-me,	KEE-LO-GRAH-M,	kilogram.
La-bo-ra-toi-re,	LAH-BO-RAH-TWAR,	laboratory.
Ma-cro-cé-pha-le,	MAH-KRO-SAY-FAH-L,	with a long head.
Na-vi-cu-lai-re,	NAH-VEE-KU-LAIR,	navicular.
l'O-bli-qui-té,	LO-BLEE-KEE-TAY,	the obliquity.
Pé-né-tra-bi-li-té,	PAY-NAY-TRAH-BEE-LEE-TAY,	penetrability.
Que-rel-leur,	KUH-REL-HER,	squabbler.
Ra-fraî-chir,	RAF-RAY-SHEER,	to cool.
Soup-çon-ner,	SOOP-SO-NAY.	to suspect.
Trans-mis-si-bi-li-té,	TRANS-MEE-SEE-BEE-LEE-TAY,	transmissibility.
U-ni-lo-cu-laire,	U-NEE-LO-KU-LAIR,	unicular.
Va-gue-mes-tre,	VAHG-MESS-TRR,	baggage-master.

French.	Pronunciation.	Translation.
Xi-lo-gra-phie,	GZE-LO-GRAH-FEE,	xilography.
Y-pré-an,	E-PRAY-O,	ypre elm.
Zé-ro-ni-que,	ZAY-RO-NEEK,	zeronic.

NASAL SOUNDS.
Lesson V.

M and *n* are sounded nasal, except when doubled or immediately followed by a vowel.

Pronounce am, an, ean, em, en,* like *an* in w*an*t.
" im, in, aim, ain, like *an* in fr*an*k.
" om, on, like *on* in l*on*g.
" um, un, nearly like *un* in gr*un*t.

Exercise.

	French.	Pronunciation.	Translation.
am,	*am*-bler,	ÄN-BLAY,	to amble.
"	*am*-bre,	ÄN-BRR,	amber.
"	fl*am*-beau,	FLÄN-BO,	torch.
an,	*an*-cre,	ÄN-KRR,	anchor.
"	d*an*s,	DÄN,	in.
"	sa-v*an*t,	SAH-VÄN,	learned man.
ean,	m*an*-ge*an*t,	MÄN-ZHÄN,	eating.
"	ch*an*-ge*an*t,	SHÄN-ZHÄN,	changeable.
em,	*em*-bar-quer,	ÄN-BAR-KAY,	to embark.
"	m*em*-bre,	MÄN-BRR,	limb.
"	t*em*ps,	TÄN,	weather.
en,	v*en*t,	VÄN,	wind.
"	*en*-fant,	ÄN-FÄN,	child.
"	fro-m*en*t,	FRO-MÄN,	wheat.

Pronounced like *an* in w*an*t.

---

* *En* is silent in verbs at the third person of plural, and it is pronounced like *an* in fr*an*k when preceded by the vowel *i*, as mien, *mine*.

DUQUET'S METHOD.

	French.	Pronunciation.	Translation.
im,	t*im*-bre,	TĂN-BRR,	stamps.
"	*im*-bé-ci-le,	ĂN-BAY-SEEL,	stupid.
"	s*im*-ple,	SĂN-PL,	simple.
in,	cr*in*,	KRĂN,	hair.
"	car-m*in*,	KARR-MĂN,	crimson.
"	*in*-fi-dè-le,	ĂN-FEE-DAI-L,	faithless.
aim,	f*aim*,	FĂN,	hunger.
"	d*aim*,	DĂN,	deer.
ain,	p*ain*,	PĂN,	bread.
"	de-m*ain*,	DUH-MĂN,	to-morrow.
"	é-cri-v*ain*,	A-KREE-VĂN,	writer.

(Pronounced like an *in* frank.*)*

om,	n*om*,	NŎN,	name.
"	*om*-bre,	ŎN-BRR,	shade.
"	t*om*-ber,	TŎN-BAY,	to fall.
on,	d*on*,	DŎN,	gift.
"	*on*-de,	ŎN-D,	wave.
"	m*on*-tre,	MŎN-TRR,	watch.

(Pronounced like on *in* long.*)*

um,	par-f*um*,	PAR-FŬN,	perfume.
"	h*um*-ble,	ŬN-BLE,	humble,
"	h*um*-ble-m*en*t,	ŬN-BLUH-MĂN,	humbly.
un,	al*un*,	AH-LŬN,	alum.
"	l*un*-di,	LŬN-DEE,	Monday.
"	*em*-pr*un*-ter,	ĂN-PRŬN-TAY,	to borrow.

(Pronounced like un *in* grunt.*)*

3

Lesson VI.

LIQUID SOUNDS.

The liquid sounds of *l*, *ll* and *gn* are, I am inclined to think, the sweetest sounds in the French language, and ought not to be neglected in speaking French, as is so often done by many persons.

l single is always liquid in words ending in ail, euil, eil and ouil.

ll double are also invariably liquid in words having aille, euille, eille and ouille, medial or final.

ill, placed as medial or final sounds, is also liquid in many words; but there are several exceptions.

1. *ll* are sounded hard in all proper names, as Del*ll*e.
2. In names of cities, as Li*ll*e.
3. In the adjectives m*ill*e, *thousand;* tranqu*ill*e, *tranquil.*
4. In the substantives v*ill*e, *town;* m*ill*e, *mile;* pup*ill*e, *pupil;* siby*ll*e, *sybil;* vaudev*ill*e, *song.*

Lesson VII.

l and *ll* liquid.

Pronounce ail and aill like eye.
" eil and eill like āye.
" euill and euill like uh-ĭ.
" ouil and ouill like ou-ĭ.
" il and ill like ee-ĭ.

DUQUET'S METHOD. 27

Exercise.

		French.	Pronunciation.	Translation.
Pronounced like eye.	ail,	tra-v*ail*,	TRAHV-EYE,	work.
	"	por-t*ail*,	PORT-EYE,	portal.
	"	gou-ver-n*ail*,	GOOV-AIR-N-EYE,	helm.
	aill,	ca-n*aille*,	KAN-EYE,	rabble.
	"	tra-v*aill*-ant,	TRAHV-EYE-ÄN,	working man.
	"	ba-t*aill*-er,	BAT-EYE-Ā,	to battle.
Pronounced like āye.	eil,	pa-r*eil*,	PAR-ĀYE,	alike.
	"	so-l*eil*,	SOL-ĀYE,	sun.
	"	ré-v*eil*,	RAYV-ĀYE,	awaking.
	eill,	cor-b*eille*,	KORB-ĀYE,	basket.
	"	vi-*eill*-esse,	VEE-ĀYE-SS,	old age.
	"	ré-v*eille*-ma-tin,	RAYV-ĀYE-MAH-TĂN,	alarm-clock.
Pron. like uh-ï.	euil,	s*euil*,	SUH-Ï,	threshold.
	"	d*euil*,	DUH-Ï,	mourning.
	euill,	f*euille*.	FUH-Ï,	leaf.
	"	f*euill*-ère,	FUH-EE-AIR,	vein of earth.

	French.	Pronunciation.	Translation.
Pronounced like *ou-ï*. { ouil,	fe-n*ouil*,	FUH-NOU-Ï,	fennel.
ouill,	gre-n*ouille*,	GRUH-NOU-Ï,	frog.
"	s*ouill*-er,	SOU-EE-A,	to soil.
"	b*ouill*-on-ne-ment,	BOU-EE-ON-MÄN,	boiling.
Pronounced like *ee-ï*. { il,	m*il*,	MEE-Ï,	millet.
"	gré-s*il*,	GRAY-ZEE-Ï,	sleet.
"	gen-t*il*-hom-me,	ZHÄN-TEE-ÏO-M,	nobleman.
ill,	f*ill*e,	FEE-Ï,	girl.
"	che-v*ill*e,	SHUH-VEE-Ï,	bolt.
"	br*ill*-am-mant,	BREE-ÏA-MÄN,	brilliantly.

LESSON VIII.

gn liquid.

gn is sounded liquid, medial or final, except in all the words having *stag, steg, stig,* as *stag*nant. *gn* beginning a word is also not sounded liquid, as *gn*ome, *gnome;* *gn*aphalium, *gnaphalium.*

Exercise.

gna, gne, gni, gny, gno, gnu.

Pronounce *gn* liquid like *gn* in mi*gn*onette.

DUQUET'S METHOD. 29

	French.	Pronunciation.	Translation.
gna,	il sai-*gna*,	EEL SAY-GNAH,	he bled.
"	il poi-*gna*,	EEL PO-GNAH,	he grasped.
"	plai-*gn*ant,	PLAY-GNÄN,	pitying.
gne,	ba-*gne*,	BÄ-GN,	prison.
"	pei-*gn*er,	PAY-GNAY,	to comb.
"	en-sei-*gne*-ment,	ÄN-SAY-GNUH MÄN,	teaching.
gni, y,	il pei-*gn*it,	EEL PAY-GNEE,	he painted.
"	Co-li-*gny*,	KO-LEE-GNEE,	Coligny.
gno,	lor-*gn*on,	LOR-GNŎN,	eye-glass.
"	i-*gno*-ble,	E-GNŎ-BL,	ignoble,
gnu,	é-gra-ti-*gn*u-re,	A-GRAH-TEE-GNUR,	scratch.

LESSON IX.

CONNECTION OF WORDS, AND PAUSES.

The reader must never forget to join the final consonant of a word to the initial vowel or *h* mute of the next word, if the first is necessarily followed by the other, as le*s* hommes, mauvai*s* enfants, o*n* a. The final consonant of articles, adjectives, pronouns and prepositions is joined to the initial vowel or *h* mute of the next word. The final consonant of the following words is always carried to the initial vowel or *h* mute of the next word: le*s*, de*s*, au*x*, u*n*, me*s*, te*s*, ce*s*, se*s*, mo*n*, to*n*, so*n*, no*s*, vo*s*, leur*s*, que*l*, aucu*n*, ce*t*, deu*x*, trois, cin*q*, si*x*, sep*t*, hui*t*, neu*f*, di*x*, ving*t*, o*n*, tou*t*, i*l*, il*s*, nou*s*, vou*s*, elles, gros,

3*

grand, petit, mauvais, bon, quand, pas, très, bien, trop, rien, beaucoup, en, sans, avec, chez, après, dès, mais, dans, plus.

The Pauses

are rendered practical by counting 1 for the comma; 1, 2, for the semicolon; 1, 2, 3, for the colon; 1, 2, 3, 4, for the period and other signs. Pause also one second before the prepositions and conjunctions, before *qui* when subjective, and *que, dont* and other objective relative pronouns.

READING LESSONS AND TRANSLATION.

READING LESSONS.

Souvenir d'une nuit à Sorrente.

1. On était au mois de Mai, aux plus beaux jours d'Italie. Il y avait quelque temps que j'étais à Rome. J'étais lassé d'une solitude aussi sévère que celle de la Ville-Eternelle. Un changement m'était indispensable. Je partis pour Naples.

2. L'absence du pays donne un besoin incessant de changement et d'émotions nouvelles, qu'il est bon de satisfaire, pour éviter le mal du pays. Les affections naturelles du cœur ont besoin d'avoir leur cour comme les eaux d'un ruisseau, qui se corrompent, quand elles cessent de glisser sur la pente qui les entraîne, ou sous le souffle de la brise qui les berce.

3. Les plaisirs de l'imagination ne suffisent pas à l'homme; quand une fois il a été heureux dans son cœur, il cherche partout ce bonheur absent. Qui le dirait? Non seulement l'ivresse des sens ne remplace pas le bonheur, mais elle l'appelle; et l'on cherche encore son pays sous le ciel de Naples et de Sorrente. Au-delà des horizons les plus enchantés, de la nature la plus riante, des rivages les plus célèbres, on aperçoit toujours la terre où l'on a commencé à vivre et à aimer. Là est toujours le plus beau pays du monde.

4. Un de mes premiers soins, en touchant à Naples, fut d'aller contempler la ville d'un lieu élevé,

TRANSLATION.

Remembrance of a night at Sorrento.

1. It was in the month of May, on the most beautiful of Italian days. I had been at Rome some time, and had become weary of a solitude so severe as that of the Eternal City. A change was indispensable. I started for Naples.

2. Absence from our country produces a constant need of change and new emotions, that must be satisfied to avoid loneliness. The natural affections of the heart must have their course, or they become disturbed, as the waters of a brook become impure when they cease to flow down the declivity that impels them, or under the breath of the wind that fans them.

3. The pleasures of imagination do not suffice man after he has once attained the happiness of his heart; he seeks everywhere this absent happiness. Who would confess it? Intoxication of the senses does not afford him enjoyment; it only invites it; and one still seeks his country under the sky of Naples and Sorrento. Beyond horizons the most beautiful, nature the most delightful, and shores the most celebrated, we see ever the land where we first lived and loved. There is always the most beautiful country in the world.

4. One of my first cares, on landing at Naples, was to view the city from an elevated place, and I

et je montai au château-St.-Elme, ou Chartreuse Saint Martin. Je partis ensuite pour Sorrente, où j'arrivai après le coucher du soleil. Le jour s'éteignait dans une nuit délicieuse; la mer dormait, le ciel se chargeait d'étoiles, et de nouvelles lumières semblaient s'attacher de temps en temps aux flancs des montagnes qui bordent le Golfe de Naples. La lune, déjà levée derrière la presqu'île de la Campanella, se mirait dans l'ombre noire que projetaient sur la mer des bosquets de lauriers. Quelle heure pour saluer le berceau du Tasse! Car c'est a Sorrente que naquit le grand poète.

5. La maison qu'il habitait occupe le point le plus charmant de la ville. Retirée au fond d'un jardin, elle domine un rocher couvert d'orangers et de lauriers, et semble se pencher au-dessus de la mer, qui l'embrasse presqu'entièrement, et murmure à ses pieds. Le propriétaire de cette demeure pour le plaisir des voyageurs, ou pour exploiter cette mine de gloire, l'a réduite en hôtel, au moins durant une saison de l'année. Libre a chacun de penser si c'est se montrer respectueux envers la mémoire d'un si beau génie! Les Napolitains sont légers et heureux; ils sont ingrats.

6. Le Tasse n'a pas un monument digne sur tout le sol de l'Italie; et le toit qui vit naître un enfant si plein d'espérance et de gloire future pour son pays, est devenu la chose de tout le monde. Heureusement que si un voyageur indifférent vient manger et

ascended to the chateau St. Elme, or Chatreuse Saint Martin. Then I started for Sorrento, where I arrived after sunset. Day had died away in a delicious night; the sea was quiet, the heavens were decked with stars, and new lights seemed to fasten themselves from time to time to the sides of the mountains that bordered the Gulf of Naples. The moon, already risen above the peninsula of Campanella, was reflected in the dark shadow, the groves of laurels cast upon the sea. What an hour to salute the cradle of Tasso! For it was at Sorrento the great poet was born.

5. The house he inhabited is situated on the most charming spot in the city. Secluded in the depths of a garden, it towers over a rock covered with orange and laurel trees; and seems to hang above the sea, which nearly surrounds it and murmurs at its feet. The proprietor of this dwelling, for the pleasure of travelers, or to take advantage of this wonder of glory, has reduced it to a hotel, at least during a certain portion of the year. Every one may judge if this appears respectful to the memory of so fine a genius. The Neapolitans are frivolous and inconstant; they are even ungrateful.

6. Tasso has no monument worthy of him on the soil of Italy; and the roof which saw the birth of a child so full of hope and future glory for his country, has become the property of every body. Happily, if an indifferent traveler comes to eat and sleep under

dormir sous ce toit, sans autre intention que celle d'y faire bonne vie, d'autres y viennent déposer un tribut d'admiration, un soupir d'amitié, et peut-être une larme. Les poètes ont des amis au-delà des âges, aussi tendres que ceux qu'ils pressaient sur leur cœur.

7. Il y avait peu d'étrangers à Sorrente. Je trouvai donc à me loger sous le toît du Tasse ; et la nuit que j'y ai passée m'est restée en mémoire avec mes plus charmantes images d'Italie. Après le repas et quelques causeries, je me retirai sur la terrasse qui domine la mer, pour jouir du frais et du repos du soir. On goûte si bien le soir en Italie, après ces long jours de soleil et d'accablement! Il y a tant de calme, de silence et de fraîcheur dans l'atmosphère! Aucun de ces bruits criards qui nous poursuivent dans les villes d'Amérique, jusqu'au milieu du sommeil ; rien de cette chaleur d'étuve qui nous cuit encore lontemps après le coucher du soleil. On se repose au milieu d'un repos universel ; c'est une jouissance parfaite.

8. Ce soir là l'air frais circulait dans les lauriers, répandant à l'entour leur parfum ; rien ne passait sur les eaux que l'image de la lune ; le tableau pittoresque de la petite ville se dessinait parfaitement sous son voile de nuit. Un vieux buste du Tasse, à demi recouvert par une feuillée de lierre, s'élevait sur le mur, et semblait contempler avec nous les charmes de cette solitude. Pauvre Tasse ! pensai-je, combien

this roof without other intention than to enjoy himself, others come there to offer a tribute of admiration, a sigh of friendship, and perhaps a tear. The poets have friends, after ages have elapsed, as tender as those whom they have pressed to their bosoms.

7. There were few strangers at Sorrento. I was able, therefore, to obtain lodging under the roof of Tasso; and the night that I passed there remains in my memory among the most delightful pictures of Italy. After supper and a little conversation, I retired to the terrace that overlooked the sea, to enjoy the coolness and repose of evening. One delights so much in the evenings of Italy, after those long days of sunshine and languor! There is so much calm, silence and freshness in the atmosphere.! None of those shrill sounds which annoy you, in the cities of America, even in the midst of sleep; none of that stifling air which roasts you yet a long time after the sun has set. One rests in the midst of universal repose; it is complete enjoyment.

8. This evening the cool air fluttered through the laurels, diffusiṅg all around their fragrance; nothing passed over the water but the image of the moon; the romantic picture of the little city was delineated perfectly under the veil of night. An old bust of Tasso, half draped with the foliage of the ivy, hung upon the wall, and seemed to contemplate with us the charms of solitude. Poor Tasso! thought I, how

ce lieu charmant dût inspirer de douces rêveries à ta jeune imagination, et faire naître dans ton âme de brûlantes inspirations! La carrière de la vie doit paraître bien enchantée, quand on la voit s'ouvrir devant soi, sous ce ciel ardent, dans cet air embaumé, au milieu de ces jardins toujours fleuris, devant cette perspective de mer, de montagnes et d'horizons vaporeux! Et cependant tu fus malheureux!

9. A peine sorti de l'enfance, à l'aurore de la gloire, au sein des délices d'une cour charmante, un sentiment pur mais impossible vint fourvoyer son cœur et saturer sa vie d'amertume. Son âme avait pu monter si haut; il crut que son cœur pourrait bien tenter d'arriver au pied d'un petit trône. Il connaissait peu la terre. Les trônes sont fait de matière; et on ne les conquérait, alors surtout, qu'avec l'épée ou de vigoureux moyens politiques; non pas avec des pensées sublimes et des sentiments célestes. Les grands le désiraient bien comme convive à leurs banquets, comme le plus bel ornement de leurs fêtes, mais comme fiancé de leur fille! . . . Voilà quelle fut sa *folie*.

10. Malade dans son âme, égaré dans sa passion malheureuse, on l'emprisonna pendant sept· ans, comme un fou malfaisant. Relâché dans un état de santé déplorable, ce *fou* donne au monde sa Jérusalem délivrée. Après, il va d'un lieu à un autre, cherchant vainement un bonheur enfui, et une santé qui ne revient plus. Enfin, lassé, il ter-

many sweet dreams of thy young imagination has this beautiful place inspired, and how many ardent sentiments has it caused to rise in thy soul! The course of life ought to appear very enchanting when we see it open before us under this glowing sky, in this perfumed air, in the midst of these gardens always blooming, opposite this view of sea, of mountains and of misty horizons. And yet thou wast unhappy.

9. Hardly emerged from childhood, in the dawn of glory, embosomed in the delights of a charming court, a sentiment pure but impossible just led astray his heart and filled his life with bitterness. His soul had mounted so high, he thought his heart could well attempt to reach the foot of a little throne. He little knew the world. Thrones are made of matter; and we can conquer them only with the sword or vigorous political means; not with sublime thought and celestial sentiments. The great were very desirous of him, as a guest at their banquets, as the most beautiful ornament of their feasts; but as the betrothed of their daughter! . . . Behold what was his *folly*.

10. Diseased in his mind, deluded in his passion, they imprisoned him for seven years as a dangerous *madman*. Released in a state of deplorable health, this *madman* gave to the world his Jerusalem delivered. Afterward he wandered from one place to another, seeking vainly lost happiness and health

mine à Rome, dans la solitude d'un cloître, au milieu d'un hôpital, ses cinquante années d'espérances déçues. Le lendemain de sa mort, la ville entière vint couronner ses restes et les porter en triomphe . . . dans la terre. Le Tasse était devenu immortel pour les hommes comme pour le ciel. Les vivants ont d'étranges flatteries en réserve pour ceux qui veulent donner des charmes à leur existence.

11. Le lendemain de cette belle nuit passée dans la maison du Tasse, je laissai à regret Sorrente, ses jardins embaumés, ses ombrages de lauriers; et, après avoir continué ma pérégrination pendant plusieurs jours, dans les montagnes et sur le Golfe de Salerne, visitant Castellamare, Amalfi, Salerne et plusieurs petits bourgs, jetés au sommet des rochers, ou cachés au fond des vallons, je dis un dernier adieu à cette belle terre d'Italie.

that would never more return. At last, worn out, he closed at Rome, in the silence of a cloister, in the midst of a hospital, his fifty years of distracted longings. The day after his death, the entire city came to crown his remains and bear them in triumph . . . to the tomb. Tasso had become immortal for men as well as for heaven. The living have strange flatteries in reserve for those who would give charms to their existence.

11. On the morrow of this beautiful night passed in the house of Tasso, I left, with regret, Sorrento, her perfumed gardens, her groves of laurels; and, after continuing my journey for several days in the mountains and about the Gulf of Salerno, visiting Castellamare, Amalfi, Salerno, and several little hamlets tossed upon the summit of cliffs, or hidden in the depths of valleys, I took a last farewell of the beautiful land of Italy.

À la Muse.

1.

Vierge, qui présidez aux accords de la lyre,
Aimez-vous, quand le jour, à son déclin, se mire
    Dans des flots de pourpre et de feu,
Sous l'ombre des grands bois, sur le flanc des montagnes,
Aimez-vous, loin du bruit, dans les vertes campagnes,
    A jouir des œuvres de Dieu ?

2.

Laissez-moi vous y suivre !... Errant à l'aventure,
Par les tableaux riants dont s'orne la nature,
    Je sais égayer mes loisirs ...
Et sans cesse bercé de mille fantaisies,
Je puise, en me jouant, mes humbles poésies
    À la source de mes plaisirs.

3.

Le joyeux écureuil courant de branche en branche,
Et sautillant du chêne au bouleau que se penche
    Pour abriter un nid d'oiseaux,
Rappelle un souvenir de mes tendres années,
Fugitives lueurs par le temps entrainées,
    Comme la feuille au bord des eaux.

To the Muse.

1.

O virgin, who presidest over the harmony of the lyre, do you love, when day at her decline embellishes herself in waves of purple and gold, in the shade of deep forests, upon the side of the mountains, far from noise in the green fields, do you love to enjoy the works of God?

2.

Let me follow you there! Wandering for adventure among the smiling pictures wherewith nature decks herself, I can enliven my leisure, and, beguiled unceasingly by a thousand fancies, draw with facility my humble rhymes from the fount of pleasure.

3.

The happy squirrel, running from branch to branch, and jumping from oak to birch tree, that droops to shelter a nest of birds, recalls a memory of my tender youth, a fugitive gleam from fleeting time, like a leaf on the shore of the sea.

4.

Parfois, du rossignol le séduisant ramage
Laisse dans mon esprit la gracieuse image
   D'un ange exhalant son amour . . .
Ces sons harmonieux resonnent dans mon âme
Comme au pied des autels une voix qui réclame
   L'espoir d'un plus heureux séjour.

5.

Pour moi le bruit du vent, le soupir de la brise
C'est un long cri de deuil, c'est un cœur qui se brise
   Déshérité par le malheur;
Le ruisseau murmurant qui bondit et m'enchante,
C'est le bonheur qui rit, c'est un hymne qui chante
   Les louanges du Créateur.

6.

Lorsque de fleurs, un jour, j'emplissais ma corbeille . . .
Je poursuivais mon rêve . . . une mouche, une abeille
   Vint bourdonner à mes côtés.
En vain j'offre à ses yeux ma moisson d'églantines,
L'ingrate agite encor ses ailes argentines
   Et fuit mes importunités.

7.

Piqué de ses refus et pour mieux la surprendre,
En courant je la suis à travers le méandre
   De son essor capricieux;

4.

Sometimes the entrancing warbling of the nightingale leaves in my heart the graceful image of an angel breathing her love; these harmonious sounds re-echo in my soul, as a voice from the foot of the altar, imploring a happier home.

5.

For me, the roar of the wind, the sigh of the breeze, is a long wail of anguish, the breaking of a heart abandoned to sorrow. The murmuring brook, which ripples and enchants me, is a song of happiness, a hymn of praise to the Creator.

6.

One day, as I was filling my basket with flowers, and pursuing my dream, a bee came buzzing at my side. In vain I tempted her eyes with my garland of eglantines; the thankless insect still fluttered her silvery wings, and fled my importunities.

7.

Piqued by her refusal, and the better to catch her, running I pursue through the meanderings of her capricious journey; but, in the distance,

Mais au loin si son vol s'arrête et se repose,
Ce n'est pas pour goûter de l'oeillet, de la rose
   Les arômes délicieux.

8.

Mais voici qu'une fleur et plus belle et plus rare,
Un suave parfum dont Dieu même est avare
   Enfin captive tous ses vœux.
C'en est fait; pour toujours la mouche industrieuse
A juré de l'aimer et s'abat plus heureuse
   Que tout ce qui vit sous les cieux.

9.

Et, peu discret témoin de sa vive allégresse,
Pensif, je me disais: "De tout ce qui le blesse
   Qu'ainsi mon espoir soit vainqueur!"
Et je crus deviner . . . muse, vous le dirais-je?
Dans ses chastes ébats, dans son gentil manège,
   Tous les mystères de mon cœur.

10.

J'y trouve le secret de ces heures perdues
Où de tant de beautés en tout lieu repandues
   J'osai négliger les attraits;
Où tant d'êtres charmants dans les champ de la vie
Ont si souvent fait naître un murmure d'envie
   Sans fixer mes regards distraits.

if she arrests her flight and reposes, it is not to taste the delicious aroma of the sweet-william or rose.

8.

But, behold! a flower rarer and more beautiful, a sweet perfume of which God himself is sparing, at length captivates all her heart. It is all over; the industrious bee has sworn to love it forever, and she alights happier than all who live beneath the heavens.

9.

And I, unwary witness of her lively joy, say to myself, thoughtfully: "May thus my hope be conqueror over all that opposes it." And I think, O Muse! to you will I confess it, in her pure pastimes and gentle tenderness, I divine all the mysteries of my heart.

10.

I find there the secret of those lost hours in which I dared neglect the attractions of so much loveliness scattered everywhere, in which so many charming beings in the field of life have so often called forth a murmur of weariness, without catching my heedless eye.

11.

De mes souhaits constants j'y vois le doux emblême ;
Seront-ils exaucés? décidez-en vous-même :
    Donnez-moi des jours de bonheur !
Soyons unis ! sous l'orme, ou sur la plage humide
Lorsque je vais songer, dans mon rêve timide,
    Je suis l'abeille et vous la fleur.

FIN DE LA DEUXIÈME PARTIE.

11.

I see there the sweet emblem of my constant wishes. Will they be consummated? Decide it yourself. Give me days of happiness! Let us be united! under the elm or on the damp sea-coast, when I fancy, in my timid dream, myself the bee and you the flower.

END OF PART SECOND.

PART THIRD.

The verb "avoir," *to have,*

Conjugated affirmatively, negatively and interrogatively, with nouns commonly used in speaking:

INDICATIF.	INDICATIVE.
Présent.	*Present.*
(Toilette, habits d'homme.)	(Gentlemen's clothes and articles used in dressing.)
1. J'ai mon chapeau.	1. I have my hat.
Je n'ai pas son habit.	I have not his coat.
Ai-je, *or* est-ce que j'ai, votre mouchoir?	Have I your handkerchief?
Tu as mon tire-bottes.	Thou hast my boot-jack.
Tu n'as pas tes bottes.	Thou hast not thy boots.
As-tu, *or* est-ce que tu as, mes bottines?	Hast thou my half-boots?
Il a un habit de chasse.	He has a hunting-coat.
Il n'a pas de manteau.	He has not any cloak.
A-t-il, *or* est-ce qu'il a, une redingote?	Has he a frock-coat?
Nous avons leurs gants.	We have their gloves.
Nous n'avons pas de paletots.	We have not any great-coats.
Avons-nous, *or* est-ce que nous avons, des guêtres?	Have we some gaiters?
Vous avez une chemise blanche.	You have a clean shirt.
Vous n'avez pas de chemises sales.	You have not any dirty shirts.
Avez-vous, *or* est-ce que vous avez, des chemises?	Have you shirts?

Ils ont des cravates.
Ils n'ont pas de bas de laine.
Ont-ils, or est-ce qu'ils ont, des caleçons?

They have cravats.
They have not any woolen stockings.
Have they drawers?

Imparfait.

2. J'avais ma robe de chambre.
Je n'avais pas de collet.
Avais-je des manchettes?
Tu avais un pantalon.
Tu n'avais pas de pantoufles.
Avais-tu des souliers?
Il avait un habit complet.
Il n'avait pas de chaussettes.
Avait-il une garniture?
Nous avions des bretelles.
Nous n'avions pas une boucle.
Avions-nous des boutons?
Vous aviez sa brosse à dents?
Vous n'aviez pas ma brosse à ongles.
Avez-vous une brosse à peigne?
Ils avaient des manches.
Ils n'avaient pas de poches.
Avaient-ils des boutonnières?

Imperfect.

2. I had my dressing-gown.
I had not any collar.
Had I cuffs?
Thou hadst pantaloons.
Thou hadst not any slippers.
Hadst thou shoes?
He had a suit of clothes.
He had not any socks.
Had he a ruffle?
We had braces.
We had not a buckle.
Had we buttons?
You had his tooth-brush.
You had not my nail-brush.
Had you a comb-brush?
They had sleeves.
They had not any pockets.
Had they button-holes?

Prétérit défini.

3. J'eus une canne.
Tu eus un peigne.
Il eut un rasoir.
Nous eûmes du savon.
Vous eûtes une éponge.
Ils eurent des lunettes.

Past definite.

3. I had a cane.
Thou hadst a comb.
He had a razor.
We had soap.
You had a sponge.
They had spectacles.

Prétérit indéfini.

4. J'ai eu un cure-dents.
Je n'ai pas eu d'épée.
Ai-je eu une montre? etc.

Perfect.

4. I have had a toothpick.
I have not had any sword.
Have I had a watch? etc.

Plusqueparfait.

5. J'avais eu de la poudre dentifrice, etc.

Pluperfect.

5. I had had tooth-powder, etc.

DUQUET'S METHOD.

Prétérit antérieur.
6. J'eus eu une perruque, etc.

Past anterior.
6. I had had a wig.

Futur.
(Habits de femmes, etc.)
7. J'aurai un chapeau.
Je n'aurai pas de tablier.
Aurai-je un corsage de dessous?
Tu auras une ceinture.
Tu n'auras pas de bottines.
Auras-tu le calicot?
Elle (il) aura un bracelet.
Elle n'aura pas de pélerine.
Aura-t-elle un manteau?
Nous aurons des corsets.
Nous n'aurons pas de boucles d'oreilles.
Aurons-nous des diamants?
Vous aurez un négligé.
Vous n'aurez pas de coiffure.
Aurez-vous une toilette de ville?
Elles (ils) auront des fourrures.
Elles n'auront pas de toilette de bal.
Auront-elles des agrafes et des portes?

Future.
(Ladies' clothing, toilet, etc.)
7. I shall have a bonnet.
I shall not have any apron.
Shall I have a bodice?
Thou wilt have a belt.
Thou wilt not have any boots.
Wilt thou have calico?
She will have a bracelet.
She will not have any cape.
Will she have a cloak?
We shall have corsets.
We shall not have any ear-rings.
Shall we have diamonds?
You will have a morning-dress.
You will not have any head-dress.
Will you have a walking-dress?
They will have furs.
They will not have any ball-dress.
Will they have hooks and eyes?

Futur antérieur.
8. J'aurai eu un nécessaire, etc.

Second future.
8. I shall have had a dressing-case, etc.

CONDITIONNEL.
Présent.
9. J'aurais une toilette de soirée.
Je n'aurais pas d'éventail.
Aurais-je un volant?
Tu aurais des guêtres.
Tu n'aurais pas de jarretières.
Aurais-tu de la gaze?
Elle (il) aurait des gants.
Elle n'aurait pas de mouchoir.

CONDITIONAL.
Present.
9. I should have an evening-dress.
I should not have any fan.
Should I have a flounce?
Thou wouldst have gaiters.
Thou wouldst not have any garters.
Wouldst thou have gauze?
She would have gloves.
She would not have any handkerchief.

Aurait-elle des épingles à cheveux ? Would she have hair-pins?
Nous aurions des bijoux. We should have jewels.
Nous n'aurions pas de dentelle. We should not have any lace.
Aurions-nous du linge ? Should we have linen?
Elles (ils) auraient des colliers. They would have necklaces.
Elles n'auraient pas de filets. They would not have any nets.
Auraient-elles des bonnets de nuit? Would they have night-caps?

Passé. *Past.*

10. J'aurais eu une chemise de nuit, 10. I should have had a night-dress,
etc. etc.

IMPÉRATIF. IMPERATIVE.

11. Aie un étui à aiguilles. 11. Have a needle-case.
Qu'elle ait ce peignoir. Let her have that morning-robe.
Qu'elle n'ait pas ce mantelet. Let her not have that mantle.
Ayons nos jupons. Let us have our petticoats.
Ayez des parfums. Have some perfume.
Qu'elles aient de la pommade. Let them have some pomatum.

SUBJONCTIF. SUBJUNCTIVE.
Présent. *Present.*

12. Afin que j'aie du rouge. 12. That I may have some paint.
Je doute que tu aies une garniture I doubt whether thou hast a set of
de rubans. ribbons.
Qu'elle ait un voile ou non. Whether she has a vail or not.
Croyez-vous qu'elle ait de l'eau de Do you think that she has any rose
rose ? water?
Je ne crois pas que nous ayons I do not think that we have enough
assez de soie. of silk.
Il faut que vous ayez un autre shâle. It is necessary that you should have
 another shawl.
Il est impossible que vous ayez une It is impossible that you should
montre. have a watch.
Je ne cr, is pas qu'elles aient besoin I do not think that they want any
d'aiguilles. needles.

Parfait. *Perfect.*

13. Quoique j'aie eu un dé. 13. Although I have had a thimble.
Est-ce vrai que tu aies eu la cor- Is it true that thou hast had wed-
beille de mariage ? etc. ding presents?

Imparfait.

14. Quelque lunettes que j'eusse.

Quoique j'eusse une jupe.
Fallait-il que tu eusses des manchettes ?
Il était bien juste qu'elle eût cette broderie.
Pour que nous eussions des écharpes.
Il voulait que vous eussiez une plume.
Je serais content qu'elles eussent des pantoufles neuves.

Plusqueparfait.

15. Il attendait que j'eusse eu des perles, etc.

INFINITIF.
Présent.
16. Avoir une pelote.

Passé.
Avoir eu de la poudre.

PARTICIPE PRÉSENT.
Ayant un anneau d'or.

PARTICIPE PASSÉ.
Ayant eu un panier à ouvrage.

Imperfect.

14. Whatever spectacles I might have.

Though I had a skirt.
Was it necessary that thou shouldst have cuffs ?
It was right that she should have that embroidery.
That we might have scarfs.

He wanted you to have a plume.

I should be pleased if they had new slippers.

Pluperfect.

15. He was waiting that I had pearls, etc.

INFINITIVE.
Present.
16. To have a pin-cushion.

Past.
To have had some powder.

PRESENT PARTICIPLE.
Having a gold ring.

PAST PARTICIPLE.
Having had a work-basket.

THE CONJUGATION OF THE VERB "ÊTRE," *to be.*

INDICATIF.
Présent.
(Professions et metiers.)
1. Je suis médecin.
Je ne suis pas pharmacien.

INDICATIVE.
Present.
(Professions and trades.)
1. I am a physician.
I am not an apothecary.

Suis-je, *or* est-ce que je suis, acteur ?	Am I an actor ?
Tu es actrice.	Thou art an actress.
Tu n'es pas artiste.	Thou art not an artist.
Es-tu, *or* est-ce que tu es, auteur ?	Art thou an author ?
Il est avocat.	He is an advocate.
Il n'est pas architecte.	He is not an architect.
Est-il, *or* est-ce qu'il est, dentiste ?	Is he a dentist ?
Nous sommes ecclésiastiques.	We are clergymen.
Nous ne sommes pas maîtres de danse.	We are not dancing-masters.
Sommes-nous, *or* est-ce que nous sommes, graveurs ?	Are we engravers ?
Vous êtes dessinateur.	You are a drawer.
Vous n'êtes pas maître de dessin.	You are not a drawing-master.
N'estes-vous pas ingénieur ?	Are you not an engineer ?
Etes-vous, *or* est-ce que vous êtes, avoué ?	Are you not an attorney ?
Ils sont astronomes.	They are astronomers.
Ils ne sont pas anatomistes.	They are not anatomists.
Sont-ils, *or* est-ce qu'ils sont, historiens ?	Are they historians ?
Ne sont-ils pas grammairiens ?	Are they not grammarians ?

Prétérit indéfini. — *Perfect.*

2. J'ai été maître d'armes.	2. I have been a fencing-master.
Tu as été géomètre.	Thou hast been a geometer.
Il a été humaniste.	He has been a humanist.
Nous avons été moralistes.	We have been moralists.
Vous avez été musicien.	You have been a musician.
Ils ont été étudiants.	They have been students.

Imparfait. — *Imperfect.*

3. J'étais professeur.	3. I was a professor.
Tu étais poète.	Thou wast a poet.
Il était philosophe.	He was a philosopher.
Nous étions navigateurs.	We were navigators.
Vous étiez peintre.	You were a painter.
Ils étaient rhétoriciens.	They were rhetoricians.

Plusqueparfait. — *Pluperfect.*

4. J'avais été prédicateur.	4. I had been a preacher.
Tu avais été chirurgien.	Thou hadst been a surgeon.

Il avait été maître d'école.
Nous avions été sculpteurs.
Vous aviez été théologien.
Ils avaient été maîtres de chant.

He had been a school-master.
We had been sculptors.
You had been a theologian.
They had been singing-masters.

Pretérit défini.
5. Je fus mécanicien.
Tu fus mathématicien.
Il fut metaphysicien.
Nous fûmes naturalistes.
Vous fûtes maître de musique.
Ils furent rhétoriciens.

Past definite.
5. I was a mechanician.
Thou wast a mathematician.
He was a metaphysician.
We were naturalists.
You were a music-master.
They were rhetoricians.

Prétérit anterieur.
6. J'eus été maître d'écriture.

(No equivalent in English.)

Futur.
7. Je serai logicien.
Tu seras agent d'affaires.
Il sera banquier.
Nous serons barbiers.
Vous serez boulanger.
Ils seront bouchers.

Future.
7. I shall be a logician.
Thou wilt be a broker.
He will be a banker.
We shall be barbers.
You will be a baker.
They will be butchers.

Futur anterieur.
8. J'aurai été courtier.
Tu auras été brasseur.
Il aura été libraire.
Nous aurons été relieurs.
Vous aurez été forgeron.
Ils auront été bottiers.

Future perfect.
8. I shall have been a broker.
Thou wilt have been a brewer.
He will have been a bookseller.
We shall have been bookbinders.
You will have been a blacksmith.
They will have been boot-makers.

CONDITIONNEL.
Présent.
9. Je serais blanchisseuse.
Tu serais miroitier.

Elle serait modiste.
Nous serions emballeurs.
Vous seriez cordier.
Ils seraient cordonniers.

CONDITIONAL.
Present.
9. I should be a laundress.
Thou wouldst be a looking-glass-maker.
She would be a milliner.
We should be packers.
You would be a ropemaker.
They would be shoemakers.

Passé.
10. J'aurais été orfèvre.
Tu aurais été tailleur.
Il aurait été chaudronnier.
Nous aurions été tapissiers.
Vous auriez été horloger.
Ils auraient été marchants de vin.

Past.
10. I should have been a silversmith.
Thou wouldst have been a tailor.
He would have been a tinker.
We should have been upholsterers.
You would have been a watchmaker.
They would have been wine-merchants.

IMPÉRATIF.
11. Sois serrurier.
Qu'il soit fabricant.
Soyons maçons.
Soyez meunier.
Qu'ils soint colporteurs.

IMPERATIVE.
11. Be a locksmith.
Let him be a manufacturer.
Let us be masons.
Be a miller
Let them be peddlers.

SUBJONCTIF.
Présent.
12. Que je sois parfumeur.
Que tu sois pâtissier.
Qu'il soit plombier.
Que nous soyons chiffonnier.
Que vous soyez raffineur.
Qu'ils soient selliers.

SUBJUNCTIVE.
Present.
12. That I may be a perfumer.
That thou mayst be a pastry-cook.
That he may be a plumber.
That we may be rag-men.
That you may be a refiner.
That they may be saddlers.

Passé.
13. Quoique j'aie été berger.

On croit même que tu aies été ferblantier, etc.

Perfect.
13. Although I have been a shepherd.
They even believe that thou hast been a tinman, etc.

Imparfait.
14. Que je fusse savonnier.
Que tu fusses tanneur.
Qu'il fût tourneur.
Que nous fussions marchands de bois.
Que vous fussiez garçon.
Qu'ils fussent ouvriers.

Imperfect.
14. That I might be a soap-boiler.
That thou mightest be a tanner.
That he might be a turner.
That we might be timber-merchants.
That you might be a waiter.
That they might be workmen.

Plusqueparfait.	*Pluperfect.*
15. Plût à Dieu que j'eusse été compositeur. Il doutait qu'il eût été aubergiste, etc.	15. Would to God that I had been a compositor. He doubted whether he had been hotel-keeper, etc.
INFINITIF. *Présent.*	INFINITIVE. *Present.*
16. Être couturière.	16. To be dressmaker.
Passé.	*Past.*
N'avoir jamais été que commis.	To have never been any thing but clerk.
PARTICIPE PRÉSENT.	PRESENT PARTICIPLE.
Etant bon menusier, il réussit.	Being a good joiner, he succeeded.
PARTICIPE PASSÉ.	PAST PARTICIPLE.
Ayant été un des meilleurs chapeliers de la ville de New York, il doit nécessairement réussir ici.	Having been one of the best hatters of the city of New York, he must necessarily succeed here.

REMARK.—The verb "avoir," *to have*, is used in the following sentences instead of the verb "être," *to be*, which is used in the same sentences when in English: j'*ai* faim, I *am* hungry; j'*ai* chaud, I *am* warm; j'*ai* froid, I *am* cold; j'*ai* sommeil, I *am* sleepy; j'*ai* raison, I *am* right; j'*ai* tort, I *am* wrong; J'*ai* peur, I *am* afraid; j'*ai* honte, I *am* ashamed.

The Gender of Nouns.

Masculine Gender.

NOUNS ending with a consonant are generally masculine, except those ending in *ion*. NOUNS ending in *ier* and *aire* are also masculine. Ex. port*ier*, proprié*taire*.

Feminine Gender.

Nouns ending with an *e* mute are generally feminine, except those ending in *aire*. Substantives ending in *ion* and *ère* are feminine. Ex. révolut*ion*, riv*ière*. Bast*ion* and p*ère* are masculine.

Articles.

Put le, *the*, before masculine nouns, singular number, and commencing with a consonant. Ex. *le* crayon, *the pencil.*

Put la, *the*, before feminine nouns, singular number, and beginning with a consonant. Ex. *la* table, *the table.*

Put l', *the*, before nouns of both genders, singular number, and commencing with a vowel or an *h* mute. Ex. *l'h*omme, *the man; l'a*rbre, *the tree.*

Put les, *the*, before nouns of both genders, plural number, and beginning with a consonant, a vowel, or an *h* mute. Ex. *les* plumes, *the pens; les* hommes, *the men; les* arbres, *the trees.*

Put du, *some*, before masculine nouns, singular number, and commencing with a consonant. Ex. *du* pain, *some bread.*

Put de l', *some, of the*, before nouns of both genders, singular number, and commencing with a vowel or an *h* mute. Ex. *de l'*argent, *some money; de l'h*omme, *of the man.*

Put au, *to the,* before masculine nouns, singular number, and commencing with a consonant. Ex. *au* lac, *to the lake.*

Put à l', *to the,* before nouns of both genders, singular number, and commencing with a vowel or an *h* mute. Ex. *à l'*homme, *to the man.*

Put aux, *to the;* des, *some, of the;* before nouns of both genders, plural number, and commencing with whatever letter. Ex. *aux* dames, *to the ladies; des* arbres, *some* or *of the trees.*

Put un, *a, an,* before masculine nouns, singular number.

Put une, *a, an,* before feminine nouns, singular number.

Determinative Adjectives.

Put mon, *my;* ton, *thy;* son, *his, her, its;* before masculine nouns, singular number, and also before feminine nouns beginning with a vowel or an *h* mute. Ex. *mon* âme, *my soul; ton* chien, *thy dog; son* chapeau, *his, her* or *its hat.*

Put ma, *my;* ta, *thy;* sa, *his, her, its;* before feminine nouns, singular number, and commencing with a consonant. Ex. *ma* sœur, *my sister; ta* cousine, *thy cousin; sa* mère, *his, her* or *its mother.*

Put mes, *my;* tes, *thy;* ses, *his, her, its;* ces, *these;* before nouns of both genders, plural number. Ex.

mes gants, *my gloves;* tes plumes, *thy pens;* ses livres, *his, her* or *its books;* ces livres, *these books.*

Put notre, *our;* votre, *your;* leur, *their;* before masculine and feminine nouns, singular number. Ex. *notre* lampe, *our lamp;* *leur* crayon, *their pencil.*

Put nos, *our;* vos, *your;* leurs, *their;* before nouns of both genders, plural number. Ex. *nos* chats, *our cats;* *vos* bottes, *your boots;* *leurs* maisons, *their houses.*

Ce, *that;* cet, *that;* cette, *that.* The first (ce) is placed before a masculine noun, singular number, and commencing with a consonant. Ex. *ce* peigne, *that comb.* The second (cet) is placed before masculine nouns, singular number, and commencing with a vowel or an *h* mute; the third (cette) before all feminine nouns, singular number. Ex. *cet h*omme, *that man;* *cette* femme, *that woman.*

How to use the Pronouns.

[The pronouns (except the personal pronouns used as subjectives) are written in italic letters]

Examples.

French.	English.
Pronoms Personnels.	Personal Pronouns.
Vous *me* (*to me*) *le* (*it* or *him*) rendrez.	You will give *it* or *him* back *to me.*
Vous ne *la* (*her* or *it*) reprendrez pas.	You will not take *her* or *it* back.

French.	English.
Je *les* (*them*) ai vues; mais elles ne *m*'ont (*m'*, *me*) pas vu.	I have seen *them;* but they have not seen *me.*
Ils parleront de *toi* (*thee*), je *t'en* (*thee of it*) averti.	They will speak of *thee*, I warn *thee of it.*
Je *lui* (*to him* or *to her*) ai parlé de *vous* (*you*).	I have spoken to *him* or to *her* of *you.*
On a souvent besoin d'un plus petit que *soi* (*himself, itself, ourselves.*)	We have often need of one more humble than *ourselves.*
Ils *se* (*himself, themselves*) flattent; mais nous ne *nous* (*ourselves*) flattons pas.	They flatter *themselves;* but we do not flatter *ourselves.*
Parlez d'*elle* (*her*), mais non pas d'*eux* (*them*, masculine).	Speak of *her,* but not of *them.*
Je suis content d'*elles* (*them*, feminine).	I am pleased with *them.*
Je *leur* (*them,* f. and m. pl.) ai dit.	I told *them.*

Pronoms Possessifs.	Possessive Pronouns.
J'ai *le mien, le tien* et *le sien* (m.)	I have *mine, thine* and *his, hers* or *its.*
As-tu *la mienne, la tienne* et *la sienne* (f.)?	Hast thou *mine, thine* and *his, hers* or *its?*
Ils avaient *les miens, les tiens* et *les siens* (m. pl.)	They had *mine, thine* and *his, hers* or *its.*

French.	English.
Elles n'ont jamais eu *les miennes, les tiennes* ou *les siennes* (f. pl.)	They never have had *mine, thine* or *his, hers* or *its.*
Nous avons *le nôtre, le vôtre* et *le leur* (m.)	We have *ours, yours* and *theirs.*
Avez-vous *la nôtre, la vôtre* et *la leur* (f.)?	Have you *ours, yours* and *theirs?*
Ils ont *les nôtres, les vôtres* et *les leurs* (f. and m. pl.)	They have *ours yours* and *theirs.*

Pronoms Démonstratifs.

Demonstrative Pronouns.

*C'*est (*c'* for *ce,* it and they) *celui* (*this* or *that*) de mon frère?	*It* is *that* of my brother.
Préferez-vous *celui-ci* (*this one,* m.) à *celui-là* (*that one,* m.)?	Do you prefer *this one* to *that one?*
Celle-ci (*this one,* f.) est meilleure que *celle-là* (*that one,* f.)	*This one* is better than *that one.*
Prenez *ceci* (*this*).	Take *this.*
Que dites-vous de *cela* (*that*)?	What do you say of *that?*
Ceux-ci (*these,* m. pl.) sont mes amis, et *ceux-là,* (*those,* m. pl.) mes ennemis.	*These* are my friends and *those,* my enemies.

French.	English.
Choisissez entre *celles-ci* (*these*, f. pl.) et *celles-là* (*those*, f. pl.)	Choose between *these* and *those*.
Je préfère *ceux* (m. pl.) ou *celles* (f. pl.) qui m'aiment.	I prefer *those* who love me.

Pronoms Relatifs. / Relative Pronouns.

Qui (*who*) vous parle?	*Who* speaks to you?
Qui (*whom*) voyez-vous?	*Whom* do you see?
Les feuilles *qui* (*which*) tombent sont mortes.	The leaves *which* fall are dead.
Les femmes *que* (*whom*) j'ai vues étaient jeunes.	The women *whom* I have seen were young.
L'argent *que* (*which*) j'ai reçu est à moi.	The money *which* I have received is mine.
Que (*what*) voulez-vous?	*What* will you have?
J'ignore ce *à quoi* il pense.	I am ignorant of *what* he thinks.
Il y avait je ne sais *quoi* dans sa main.	There was I know not *what* in his hand.
La personne *dont* (*of whom, of which, whose*, m. and f., s. and pl.) je vous ai parlé, est arrivée.	The person *of whom* I have spoken to you, has arrived.
Qu'*en* (*of it, of them, from it, from them, some, any*) pensez-vous?	What do you think *of it* or *of them*?

French.	English.
J'*en* suis loin.	I am far *from it* or *from them.*
J'*en* ai.	I have *some of it* or *of them.*
J'*y** (*of it, of them, to it, to them*) pensais.	I was thinking *of it* or *of them.*
J'*y* donne mes soins.	I devote my care *to it* or *to them.*
Lequel (m.), *laquelle* (f.), *lesquels* (m. pl.), *lesquelles* (f. pl.), voyez-vous?	Which one do you see?
Duquel (m.), *de laquelle* (f.), *desquels* (m. pl.), *desquelles* (f. pl.), parlez-vous?	Of which one do you speak?
Dans *lequel,* etc., je tombai.	In *which* I fell.
Auquel (m.), *à laquelle* (f.), *auxquels* (m. pl.), *auxquelles* (f. pl.), j'ai confié ma vie.	To *which* I have intrusted my life.
PRONOMS INDÉFINIS.	INDEFINITE PRONOUNS.
Ne parlez pas des défauts *d'autrui.*	Do not speak of the defects of *others.*
Chacun (every one, each one) a ses défauts.	*Every one* has his defects.

---

* Never use the pronoun *y* with regard to persons.

French.	English.
On (*one, people, they*) parle trop.	*People* speak too much.
Personne (*no one, nobody*) ne veut le prendre.	*No one* wishes to take it.
Quelqu'un (*some one, somebody*) veut vous parler.	*Somebody* wishes to speak to you.
Quiconque (*whoever, whosoever*) flatte ses maîtres, les trahit.	*Whoever* flatters his masters, betrays them.
Tout le monde se confiait *l'un à l'autre* (m.; *l'une, l'autre*, f.) cette confidence.	Every body confided *one to another* this communication.
Tout le peuple suivit Virginie, *les unes* (m. pl.; *les unes*, f. pl.) par curiosité, *les autres* (m. and f. pl.) par considération pour Icilius.	All the people followed Virginia, *some* through curiosity, *some* through respect for Icilius.
La Condamine a parcouru *l'un et l'autre* (m.; *l'une et l'autre*, f.) hemisphère.	La Condamine traveled over *both* hemispheres.
Ils se réunissaient *les uns et les autres* (m. pl.; *les unes et les autres*, f. pl.) contre l'ennemi commun.	They united *with one another* against the common enemy.

French.	English.
Tel (m. s.; *telle*, f.; *tels*, m. pl.; *telles*, f. pl.) est l'homme.	*Such* is man.
Tel est pris qui croyait prendre.	*Many* are caught while attempting to catch others.
Tout (*every one, every thing, all*) va bien.	*All* goes well.

COUNTING.

French.	English.
Nombres cardinaux.	*Cardinal numbers.*
Un, une, *f.*	One.
Deux.	Two.
Trois.	Three.
Quatre.	Four.
Cinq.	Five.
Six.	Six.
Sept.	Seven.
Huit.	Eight.
Neuf.	Nine.
Dix.	Ten.
Onze.	Eleven.
Douze.	Twelve.
Treize.	Thirteen.
Quatorze.	Fourteen.
Quinze.	Fifteen.
Seize.	Sixteen.
Dix-sept.	Seventeen.

French.	English.
Dix-huit.	Eighteen.
Dix-neuf.	Nineteen.
Vingt.	Twenty.
Vingt et un.	Twenty-one.
Vingt-deux.	Twenty-two.
Vingt-trois.	Twenty-three.
Vingt-quatre.	Twenty-four.
Vingt-cinq.	Twenty-five.
Vingt-six.	Twenty-six.
Vingt-sept.	Twenty-seven.
Vingt-huit.	Twenty-eight.
Vingt-neuf.	Twenty-nine.
Trente.	Thirty.
Trente et un.	Thirty-one.
Trente-deux.	Thirty-two.
Trente-trois, etc.	Thirty-three, etc.
Quarante.	Forty.
Cinquante.	Fifty.
Soixante.	Sixty.
Soixante-dix.	Seventy.
Soixante et onze.	Seventy-one.
Soixante-douze.	Seventy-two.
Soixante-treize, etc.	Seventy-three, etc.
Quatre-vingts.	Eighty.
Quatre-vingt-dix.	Ninety.
Quatre-vingt-onze.	Ninety-one.
Quatre-vingt-douze, etc.	Ninety-two, etc.
Cent.	A hundred.

DUQUET'S METHOD.

French.	English.
Cent-un.	A hundred and one.
Cent-deux.	A hundred and two.
Cent-trois, etc.	A hundred and three, etc.
Deux cents.	Two hundred.
Trois cents.	Three hundred.
Quatre cents.	Four hundred.
Cinq cents, etc.	Five hundred, etc.
Mille.	A thousand.
Deux mille, etc.	Two thousand, etc.
Un million.	A million.

Nombres ordinaux.	*Ordinal numbers.*
Premier.	First.
Deuxième.	Second.
Troisième.	Third.
Quatrième.	Fourth.
Cinquième.	Fifth.
Sixième.	Sixth.
Septième.	Seventh.
Huitième.	Eighth.
Neuvième.	Ninth.
Dixième.	Tenth.
Onzième.	Eleventh.
Douzième.	Twelfth.
Treizième.	Thirteenth.
Quatorzième.	Fourteenth.
Quinzième.	Fifteenth.
Seizième.	Sixteenth.

French.	English.
Dix-septième.	Seventeenth.
Dix-huitième.	Eighteenth.
Dix-neuvième.	Nineteenth.
Vingtième.	Twentieth.
Vingt-et-unième.	Twenty-first.
Vingt-deuxième.	Twenty-second.
Vingt-troisième.	Twenty-third.
Vingt-quatrième, etc.	Twenty-fourth, etc.
Trentième.	Thirtieth.
Quarantième.	Fortieth.
Cinquantième.	Fiftieth.
Soixantième.	Sixtieth.
Soixante-dixième.	Seventieth.
Quatre-vingtième.	Eightieth.
Quatre-vingt-dixième.	Ninetieth.
Centième.	Hundredth.
Cent-unième.	Hundred and first.
Cent-deuxième, etc.	Hundred and second, etc.
Deux-centième, etc.	Two hundredth, etc.
Millième, etc.	Thousandth, etc.
Millionième, etc.	Millionth, etc.

Time and its Divisions.

Une seconde.	A second.
Une minute.	A minute.
Un quart d'heure.	A quarter of an hour.
Une demi-heure.	Half an hour.

French.	English.
Trois quarts d'heure.	Three quarters of an hour.
Une heure.	An hour.
Un jour, une journée.	A day.
Une semaine.	A week.
Une quinzaine.	A fortnight.
Un mois.	A month.
Un an, une année.	A year.
Un siècle.	A century.
Le matin.	The morning.
La matinée.	The forenoon.
Midi.	Noon.
L'après-midi.	The afternoon.
Le soir.	The evening.
La nuit.	The night.
Minuit.	Midnight.
Aujourd'hui.	To-day.
Demain.	To-morrow.
Après-demain,	The day after to-morrow.
La semaine prochaine.	Next week.
Le mois prochain.	Next month.
L'an prochain, l'année prochaine.	Next year.
Hier.	Yesterday.
Avant-hier.	The day before yesterday.
La veille.	The day before.
Le lever du soleil.	Sunrise.
Le coucher du soleil.	Sunset.

French.	English.
Les Jours.	*The Days.*
Dimanche.	Sunday.
Lundi.	Monday.
Mardi.	Tuesday.
Mercredi.	Wednesday.
Jeudi.	Thursday.
Vendredi.	Friday.
Samedi.	Saturday.
Tous les jours.	Every day.
Les Mois.	*The Months.*
Janvier.	January.
Février.	February.
Mars.	March.
Avril.	April.
Mai.	May.
Juin.	June.
Juillet.	July.
Août (oo).	August.
Septembre.	September.
Octobre.	October.
Novembre.	November.
Décembre.	December.
Les Saisons.	*The Seasons.*
Le printemps.	The spring.
L'été.	The summer.
L'automne (lotoun).	The autumn.
L'hiver.	The winter.

French.	English.
Nations.	*Nations.*
Un Américain.	An American.
Un Allemand.	A German.
Un Algérien.	An Algerian.
Un Africain.	An African.
Un Anglais.	An Englishman.
Un Autrichien.	An Austrian.
Un Arabe.	An Arab.
Un Asiatique.	An Asiatic.
Un Bavarois.	A Bavarian.
Un Belge.	A Belgian.
Un Brésilien.	A Brazilian.
Un Bohémien.	A Bohemian.
Un Breton.	A Breton.
Un Castillan.	A Castilian.
Un Canadien.	A Canadian.
Un Chinois.	A Chinese.
Un Chilien.	A Chilian.
Un Corse.	A Corsican.
Un Danois.	A Dane.
Un Européen.	An European.
Un Écossais.	A Scotchman.
Un Égyptien.	An Egyptian.
Un Français.	A Frenchman.
Un Gaulois.	A Gaul.
Un Gallois.	A Welchman.
Un Grec.	A Greek.
Un Hanovérien.	A Hanoverian.

French.	English.
Un Hongrois.	A Hungarian.
Un Helvétien.	A Helvetian.
Un Irlandais.	An Irishman.
Un Indien.	An Indian.
Un Islandais.	An Icelander.
Un Japonais.	A Japanese.
Un Juif.	A Jew.
Un Moscovite.	A Muscovite.
Un Mexicain.	A Mexican.
Un Normand.	A Norman.
Un Napolitain.	A Neapolitan.
Un Norvégien.	A Norwegian.
Un Parisien.	A Parisian.
Un Persan.	A Persian.
Un Piémontais.	A Piedmontese.
Un Péruvien.	A Peruvian.
Un Prussien.	A Prussian.
Un Polonais.	A Pole.
Un Russe.	A Russian.
Un Saxon.	A Saxon.
Un Savoyard.	A Savoyard.
Un Sarde.	A Sardinian.
Un Sicilien.	A Sicilian.
Un Suisse.	A Swiss.
Un Suédois.	A Swede.
Un Syrien.	A Syrian.
Un Turc.	A Turk.
Un Wertembergeois.	A Wertembergian.

French.	English.
Parenté.	*Kindred.*
Les ancêtres.	The ancestors.
Un bisaïeul.	A great-grandfather.
Les descendants.	The descendants.
Un grand-père.	A grandfather.
Une grand'mère.	A grandmother.
Un père.	A father.
Une mère.	A mother.
Un mari.	A husband.
Une épouse, Un époux.	A consort.
Une femme.	A wife, woman.
Une famille.	A family.
Une fille.	A daughter, a girl.
Un fils.	A son.
Un arrière-petit-fils.	A great-grandson.
Un beau-fils.	A son-in-law, step-son.
Un beau-frère.	A brother-in-law.
Un beau-père.	A father-in-law, step-father.
Une belle-mère.	A mother-in-law, step-mother.
Une belle-fille.	A daughter-in-law, step-daughter.
Une belle-sœur.	A sister-in-law.
Un gendre.	A son-in-law.
Une bru.	A daughter-in-law.
Un petit-fils.	A grand-son.

French.	English.
Un frère.	A brother.
Une petite-fille.	A grand-daughter.
Une sœur.	A sister.
Un oncle.	An uncle.
Une tante.	An aunt.
Un cousin, Une cousine.	A cousin.
Un cousin germain, Une cousine germaine.	The first cousin.
Un parrain.	A godfather.
Une marraine.	A godmother.
Un neveu.	A nephew.
Une nièce.	A niece.
Un filleul.	A godson.
Une filleule.	A goddaughter.
Un père nourricier.	A foster father.
Une mère nourricière.	A nurse.

Parties du corps humain. *Parts of the human body.*

La tête.	The head.
Les cheveux.	The hair.
La face.	The face.
Le cerveau, la cervelle.	The brain.
Le crâne.	The skull.
Le front.	The forehead.
Les tempes.	The temples.
Les sourcils.	The eyebrows.
L'œil (yeux, pl.)	The eye.
La paupière.	The eyelid.

French.	English.
Les cils.	The eyelashes.
La prunelle.	The pupil of the eye.
Les joues.	The cheeks.
Le teint.	The complexion.
Les oreilles.	The ears.
L'ouïe.	The hearing.
Le néz.	The nose.
Les narines.	The nostrils.
La bouche.	The mouth.
Les lèvres.	The lips.
Les dents.	The teeth.
Les gencines.	The gums.
La langue.	The tongue.
Le palais.	The palate.
La gorge.	The throat.
Le menton.	The chin.
Une moustache.	A moustache.
Les favoris.	The whiskers.
La barbe.	The beard.
Le cou.	The neck.
Les épaules.	The shoulders.
Les bras.	The arms.
Le coude.	The elbow.
Les mains.	The hands.
Les doigts.	The fingers.
Le poing.	The fist.
Les ongles.	The nails.
L'index.	The forefinger.

French.	English.
Le pouce.	The thumb.
La poitrine.	The chest.
Le sein.	The bosom.
Les poumons.	The lungs.
Le cœur.	The heart.
Le foie.	The liver.
La rate.	The spleen.
Les muscles.	The muscles.
Les nerfs.	The nerves.
Les veines.	The veins.
Une artère.	An artery.
Les os.	The bones.
La moèlle.	The marrow.
Les boyaux.	The bowels.
Le dos.	The back.
L'épine dorsale.	The back-bone.
Les reins.	The loins.
Les entrailles.	The entrails.
Le corps.	The body.
Le coté.	The side.
Les hanches.	The hips.
Les cuisses.	The thighs.
Les jambes.	The legs.
Les genoux.	The knees.
La cheville.	The ankle.
Les talons.	The heels.
Les pieds.	The feet.
Le cou-de-pied.	The instep.
Les orteils.	The toes.

French.	English.
Maladies.	*Maladies.*
L'apoplexie.	Apoplexy.
Une attaque.	An attack, fit.
Un abcès.	An abscess.
Aveugle.	Blind.
L'agonie.	Agony.
Une brûlure.	A burn.
Une blessure.	A wound.
La colique.	The colic.
Une contusion.	A bruise.
Un chancre.	A cancer.
Une coupure.	A cut.
Un cor.	A corn.
Une crevasse.	A chap.
La crampe.	Cramp.
Une dislocation.	A dislocation.
Une enflure.	A swelling.
Un enrouement.	Hoarseness.
Une entorse.	A sprain.
L'épilepsie.	Epilepsy.
Un évanouissement.	Fainting.
Une égratignure.	A scratch.
La fièvre.	Fever.
La fièvre jaune.	Yellow fever.
La fièvre scarlatine.	Scarlet fever.
La fièvre intermittente.	Intermittent fever.
La fièvre inflammatoire.	Burning fever.
La fièvre quarte.	A quartan ague.

French.	English.
La fièvre maligne.	Malignant fever.
La fièvre tierce.	A tertian ague.
Une fistule.	A fistula.
Le frisson.	A chill.
La gangrène.	Gangrene.
La goutte.	The gout.
Un goître.	A throat wen.
La gravelle.	Gravel.
L'hydropisie.	Dropsy.
Une indigestion.	An indigestion.
Une infirmité.	An infirmity.
Une indisposition.	An indisposition.
La jaunisse.	Jaundice.
Une maladie.	A malady.
Un malaise.	An indisposition.
La migraine.	The migrim.
La petite-vérole.	The small-pox.
La pulmonie.	Consumption.
La paralysie.	Paralysis.
La peste.	The plague.
La pleurésie.	Pleurisy.
Un rhume.	A cold.
Un rhumatisme.	Rheumatism.
La rougeole.	The measles.
Le scorbut.	Scurvy.
La toux.	A cough.
Un ulcère.	An ulcer.
Un vertige.	Dizziness.

French.	English.
Meubles d'appartement.	*Household furniture.*
L'antichambre.	Antechamber.
Des allumettes.	Matches.
L'appartement des enfants.	Nursery.
Une assiete.	Plate.
De l'amadou.	Tinder.
Un banc.	Bench.
Un balai.	Broom.
Un bassin.	Basin.
Une boîte.	Box.
Un bureau.	Bureau.
Le bois de lit.	Bedstead.
Une brosse.	Brush.
Un berceau.	Cradle.
Le buffet.	Sideboard.
La buanderie.	Wash-house.
Du bois.	Wood.
Le chenet.	Andirons.
Les cendres.	Ashes.
Une couverture de laine.	Blanket.
Une chambre à coucher.	Bedroom.
Une carafe (bouteille).	Bottle.
Une cage.	Cage.
Un canapé.	Canopy.
Une chaise.	Chair.
Une chandelle.	Candle.
Un chandelier.	Candlestick.

French.	English.
Une cheminée.	Chimney.
Du charbon de terre.	Coal.
Du charbon de bois.	Charcoal.
Un coussin.	Cushion.
Une courte-pointe.	Counterpane.
Un cabinet.	Cabinet.
Des cartes à jouer.	Cards.
Une chambre.	Chamber.
La cave.	Cellar.
Une commode.	Chest of drawers.
Un cadre.	Frame.
La clé.	Key.
La cuisine.	Kitchen.
Un clou.	Nail.
Une cruche, pot à l'eau.	Pitcher.
La casserole.	Saucepan.
Le crachoir.	Spittoon.
Une cafetière.	Coffee-pot.
Un candélabre.	Chandelier.
Combustible.	Fuel.
Une chaudière.	Boiler.
Un coffre.	Chest.
Une corbeille.	Basket.
Un couteau.	Knife.
Une cuiller.	Spoon.
Un cuvier.	Tub.
Un drap.	Sheet.
Un essuie-main.	Towel.

French.	English.
Un entonnoir.	Funnel.
Un éteignoir.	Extinguisher.
L'escalier.	Staircase.
Une fourchette.	Fork.
Un foyer.	Hearth.
Un fourgon.	Poker.
Un fauteuil.	Arm-chair.
Un fer à repasser.	Smoothing iron.
La fenêtre.	Window.
Un garde-cendres.	Fender.
Une grille.	Grate.
Un lit.	Bed.
Literie.	Bedding.
Un lustre.	Sconce.
Une lumière.	Light.
Une lampe.	Lamp.
Un lit de plume.	Feather bed.
Une lanterne.	Lantern.
Linge de lit.	Sheeting.
Un meuble.	A piece of furniture.
Une mansarde.	Attic.
Le marteau.	Knocker.
Le miroir.	Looking-glass.
Un matelas.	Mattress.
Une marchepied.	Footstool.
Les mouchettes.	Snuffers.
Un moutardier.	Mustard-pot.
Une marche.	Step.

French.	English.
La nappe.	Tablecloth.
Une natte.	Mat.
Un oreiller.	Pillow.
Les persiennes.	Blinds.
Un panier.	Basket.
Une peinture.	A painting, picture.
Une pelle.	Shovel.
Les pincettes.	Tongs.
Une pendule.	Clock.
La porte cochère.	Gate.
Le plafond.	Ceiling.
Un poêle.	Stove.
Une poêle.	Frying-pan.
Un pot.	Kettle.
Un pupitre.	Desk.
La poivrière.	Pepper-box.
Les rideaux.	Curtains.
La rampe.	Bannisters.
Un soufflet.	Bellows.
La sonnette.	Bell.
Une salière.	Saltcellar.
Du savon.	Soap.
Une serviette.	Napkin.
Un sofa.	Sofa.
Un seau.	Pail.
Une soucoupe.	Saucer.
Une sucrier.	Sugar-dish.
Une soupière.	Soup-tureen.

French.	English.
Un secrétaire.	Desk.
Le salon.	Drawing-room.
La serrure.	Lock.
Une souricière.	Mouse-trap.
Une table.	Table.
Une table de jeu.	Card-table.
Un tire-bouchon.	Corkscrew.
Des tiroirs.	Drawers.
Les tisons.	Embers.
Un tabouret.	Footstool.
La tapisserie, la tenture.	Hangings.
Le trou de la serrure.	Key-hole.
Le toit.	Roof.
Un tableau.	Picture.
Une theière.	Tea-pot.
Une tasse.	Tea-cup.
Une tablette.	Shelf.
Un tapis.	Carpet.
Un traversin.	Bolster.
Un verre.	Glass.
Un vase.	Vase.

Plats et boissons.	*Dishes and ordinary beverages.*
De l'ale.	Ale.
Du Bordeaux.	Claret.
Du Bourgogne.	Burgundy.
De la bière.	Beer.
Du bouillon.	Broth.

French.	English.
Du bœuf.	Beef.
Du bouilli.	Boiled beef, boiled meat.
Un canard.	A duck.
Une caille.	Quail.
Des confitures.	Preserves.
Une cotelette.	Cutlet.
Du cognac.	Brandy.
Du champagne.	Champagne.
Du cidre.	Cider.
Du café.	Coffee.
De la crême.	Cream.
Du chocolat.	Chocolate.
Du dindon.	Turkey.
De l'eau.	Water.
Un gigot de mouton.	Leg of mutton.
Un jambon.	Ham.
Un lapin.	Rabbit.
Un lièvre.	Hare.
De la limonade.	Lemonade.
Du mouton.	Mutton.
Des œufs.	Eggs.
Une omelette.	Omelet.
Du punch.	Punch.
Une perdrix.	Partridge.
Du porc.	Pork.
Un pâté.	Pie.
Du poulet.	Chicken.
Du rôti.	Roast meat.

French.	English.
Des rafraîchissements.	Refreshments.
Du rhum.	Rum.
De la saucisse.	Sausage.
De la soupe maigre.	Vegetable soup.
De la soupe.	Soup.
Une tarte.	Tart.
Du thé.	Tea.
De la volaille.	Fowl.
Du vermicelle.	Vermicelli.
Du veau.	Veal.
Du vin.	Wine.
Du vin nouveau.	New wine.
Du vin vieux.	Old wine.
Du vin rouge.	Red wine.
Du vin blanc.	White wine.
Du vin de France.	French wine.
Du vin du Rhin.	Rhenish wine.
Du vin de Moselle.	Moselle.
Du vin d'Oporto.	Port.
Du vin de Xeres.	Sherry.

CONVERSATION.

Le départ.	*The departure.*
Bon jour.	Good morning.
Bon soir.	Good evening.
Bonne nuit.	Good night.
Adieu.	Adieu.

French.	English.
Bon voyage.	I wish you a pleasant journey.
Merci.	Thank you.
Où allez-vous ?	Where do you go ?
À New York.	To New York.
Quand partez-vous ?	When do you depart ?
Demain avant midi.	To-morrow forenoon.
Quand revenez-vous ?	When do you return ?
Dans un mois.	In a month.
Ne m'oubliez-pas.	Do not forget me.
Pensez à moi.	Think of me.
Ecrivez moi souvent.	Write me often.

Le temps. — *The weather.*

Il fait un temps superbe.	It is beautiful weather.
Il fait un temps désagréable.	It is disagreeable weather.
It fait bien de la crotte.	It is very dirty.
Il fait beaucoup de poussière.	It is dusty.
Je pense qu'il pleuvra.	I think it will rain.
Le temps s'éclaircit.	It is clearing up.
Il pleut.	It rains.
Il neige.	It snows.
Il gèle.	It freezes.
Il dégèle.	It thaws.
Il grêle.	It hails.
Il fait chaud.	It is warm.

French.	English.
Il fait froid.	It is cold.
Il ne fait pas trop chaud.	It is not too warm.
Il ne fait pas trop froid.	It is not too cold.

À propos de nouvelles. — About news.

French.	English.
Comment?	What?
Est-ce possible?	Is it possible?
Ce n'est pas possible!	It is impossible!
Vraiment!	You don't say so!
C'est malheureux!	It is too bad!
C'est épouvantable!	How dreadful!
Quel dommage!	What a pity!
Vous me surprenez.	You surprise me.
Je suis bien en colère.	I am very angry.
J'en suis fort content.	I am very glad of it.
Vous ne me surprenez-pas.	You do not surprise me.
Cela me fait grand plaisir.	It gives me great pleasure.
Est-ce que vous plaisantez?	Are you joking?
Que voulez-vous dire?	What do you mean?
N'importe.	Never mind.
Il faut bien que le monde parle.	People must talk.

L'âge et le nom. — Age and name.

French.	English.
Quel âge avez-vous?	How old are you?
J'ai vingt ans.	I am twenty years old.

French.	English.
Vous paraissez plus âgé *or* plus vieux.	You look older.
Vous paraissez moins âgé *or* plus jeune.	You look younger.
Comment vous appelez-vous?	What is your name?
Quel est votre nom de famille?	What is your surname?
Quel est votre nom de baptême?	What is your Christian name?

L'heure. — *The time.*

Quelle heure est-il?	What o'clock is it?
Il est trois heures.	It is three o'clock.
Il est cinq heures passées.	It is after five.
Il est cinq heures vingt-cinq.	It is twenty-five minutes past five.
Il est de bonne heure.	It is early.
Il est tard.	It is late.
Il est onze heures moins un quart.	It is a quarter to eleven.
À quelle heure déjeunez-vous?	At what hour do you breakfast?
À quelle heure dînez-vous?	At what hour do you dine?
À quelle heure prenez-vous le thé?	At what hour do you take tea?
À quelle heure vous couchez-vous?	At what hour do you go to bed?

French.	English.
Je me couche á dix heures.	I go to bed at ten.
À quelle heure vous levez-vous ?	At what hour do you rise ?
Je me lève à six heures.	I rise at six.

Santé. — Health.

Je me porte bien.	I am well.
Elle se porte à merveille.	She is perfectly well.
Madame, votre mère, est-elle mieux ?	Is your mother better ?
Qu'avez-vous ?	What is the matter with you ?
Je suis indisposé.	I am indisposed.
J'ai le mal de tête.	I have the headache.
J'ai le mal de dents.	I have the toothache.
J'ai le mal de cœur.	I have the heartache.
J'ai le mal de gorge.	I have the sore throat.
J'ai le rhume de cerveau.	I have a cold in my head.
Je suis enrhumé.	I have a cold.
Comment vous portez-vous ?	How are you ?
Je me porte mieux.	I am better.
Je suis faible.	I am weak.

Admirer. — To admire.

Je l'aime.	I love her, him *or* it.
Je l'admire.	I admire her, him *or* it.
Elle est charmante !	She is charming.

French.	English.
Quel air noble!	What a noble appearance!
Quelle grâce!	What elegance!
C'est une beauté.	It is a beauty.
Elle est belle.	She is handsome.
Elle est jolie.	She is pretty.
Quel esprit!	What a wit!
Quel génie!	What a genius!
C'est ravissant.	It is ravishing.
C'est magnifique.	It is magnificent.
C'est sublime.	It is sublime.
Quelle grandeur d'âme!	What magnanimity!
Quel énergie!	What energy!
Quel beau talent!	What a fine talent!
Quelle volonté!	What a will!
Quel courage!	What courage!
Quel goût!	What taste!
Quelle délicatesse!	What delicacy!
C'est étonnant.	It is astonishing.
Quel marveilleux spectacle!	What a wonderful spectacle!
Quelle merveille!	What a wonder!
Quelle bonté!	What goodness!
Quelle sensibilité touchante!	What a touching sensibility!
Quelle admirable simplicité!	What an admirable simplicity!
C'est un chef-d'œuvre.	It is a masterpiece.

French.	English.
Promenade.	*Walking.*
Allons à la promenade.	Let us take a walk.
Voulez-vous venir vous promener avec moi ?	Will you take a walk with me ?
Avec plaisir, merci; où irons-nous ?	With pleasure, thank you; where shall we go ?
Aux Champs-Elisés.	To the Champs-Elisés.
Marchons plus vite.	Let us walk faster.
Dépêchons-nous.	Let us make haste.
Veuillez marcher plus lentement.	Please walk more slowly.
Je suis fatigué.	I am fatigued.
Reposons-nous.	Let us rest.
Asseyons-nous sur ce siège ci.	Let us sit on this seat.
Acheter.	*To buy.*
Je desire acheter ——	I wish to buy ——
Faites m'en voir à la dernière mode.	Show me some of the latest styles.
Montrez m'en d'autres.	Show me some others.
Combien le vendez-vous ? Quel est le prix ?	What is the price of it ?
C'est trop cher.	It is too dear.
C'est bon marché.	It is cheap.
Je ne les aime pas.	I do not like them.
Je n'aime pas la forme.	I do not like the shape.

French.	English.
Je préfere celui-ci.	I prefer this one.
Envoyez le chez moi, rue ——, numéro ——.	Send it to my house, —— street, number ——.

Le chemin.	*The road.*
Voulez-vous m'indiquer le chemin qui conduit à ——?	Will you show me the road to ——?
Prenez le premier chemin à gauche.	Take the first road to your left.
Combien y a-t-il d'ici là? *or* quelle est la distance d'ici à ——?	How far is it from here to there? *or* what is the distance from here to ——?
Les chemins, sont-ils bons?	Are the roads good?
Oui, monsieur.	Yes, sir.
Non, monsieur, pas beaucoup.	No, sir, not much.

Voyage en chemin de fer.	*Railway journey.*
Quel est la prix d'ici à M.?	What is the fare from here to M.?
Donnez moi un billet de première classe.	Give me a first class ticket.
Voulez-vous pèser mon bagage?	Will you weigh my baggage?
Combien pèse-t-il?	How much does it weigh?

French.	English.
Je désire qu'il soit enrégistré jusqu'à M.	I wish to check it through to M.
Où est la voiture de M.?	Where is the car for M.?
Quand partons-nous?	When do we start?
Combien de temps s'arrête-t-on ici?	How long do we stop here?
Aurons nous le temps de dîner?	Shall we have time to dine?
Où est le buffet?	Where is the refreshment-room?
Change-t-on de voiture ici?	Do we change cars here?
Quand arriverons nous à M.?	When shall we arrive at M.?
Est-ce là M.?	Is this M.?
Où est mon bagage?	Where is my baggage?

Dans une ville.	*In a city.*
Cette rue conduit-elle à ——?	Does this street lead to ——?
Où conduit cette rue?	Where does this street lead to?
Voulez-vous m'indiquer où est la rue ——?	Will you tell me the way to —— street?
Dois-je tourner à droite où à gauche?	Do I turn to the right or to the left?
Quelle distance y a-t-il d'ici à la grande poste?	How far is it from here to the post-office?

French.	English.
Suis loin de l'Hotel de ——?	Am I far from —— Hotel?
Quelles pièces joue-t-on ce soir au théâtre de ——?	What plays are performed to-night at —— theater?
Y a-t-il un ballet ce soir?	Is there a ballet to-night?
Quel opéra donne-t-on ce soir?	What is the opera to-night?
Quelle est la prima donna?	Who is the prima donna?
Quel est le ténor?	Who is the tenor?
Qui remplit le rôle de ——?	Who acts the part of ——?
Où puis-je acheter un livret?	Where can I buy a libretto?
Quelles sont ici les plus belles églises?	What are the most beautiful churches here?
Quels sont vos principaux édifices publics?	What are your principal public buildings?
Garçon, allez me chercher un fiacre.	Waiter, go and get me a cab.
Je prendrai ce fiacre à l'heure.	I will take this cab by the hour.
Combien dois-je payer par heure?	How much do I pay an hour?
Conduisez moi à ——.	Drive me to ——.

French.	English.
Dans un café.	*In a café.*
Garçon, servez moi à dîner.	Waiter, serve me a dinner.
Voici le menu, monsieur.	Here is the bill of fare, sir.
Apportez moi une Julienne à la Colbert.	Bring me a Julienne à la Colbert.
Donnez moi du jambon aux épinards.	Give me some ham with spinach.
Servez moi le dessert.	Serve me dessert.
Quel vin prendrez-vous ?	What wine will you take ?
Donnez moi une bouteille de bière de Munich.	Give me a bottle of Munich beer.
Garçon, des cigares et des allumettes.	Waiter, bring some cigars and matches.
Avez-vous ici des journaux Anglais et Américains ?	Have you English and American newspapers here ?
Donnez moi le London Times et le New York World.	Give me the London Times and the New York World.
Invitation.	*Invitation.*
M. et Mad. —— présentent leurs compliments à M. et à Mad. ——, et les prient de leur faire l'honneur de	Mr. and Mrs. —— present their compliments to Mr. and Mrs. ——, and beg the favor of their company to din-

9

French.	English.
venir dîner avec eux Jeudi soir à sept heures.	ner next Thursday evening at seven o'clock.
Reponse.	*Answer.*
M. et Mad. —— acceptent avec plaisir l'aimable invitation à dîner de M. et de Mad. ——, et les prient d'agréer leurs compliments sincères.	Mr. and Mrs. —— present their compliments to Mr. and Mrs. ——, and have great pleasure in accepting their kind invitation to dinner.
M. et Mad. —— sont désolés de ne pouvoir se rendre à l'aimable invitation à dîner de M. et de Mad. ——.	Mr. and Mrs. —— regret that they will not be able to accept the kind invitation to dinner of Mr. and Mrs. ——.

END OF THE THIRD AND LAST PART.

ERRATA.

Page 5, Alphabet, *u,* nearly like *e,* instead of *ee,* in *her.*

Page 8, Diphthongs, *au,* not as broad as *oh,* instead of *ah.*

www.ingramcontent.com/pod-product-compliance
Lightning Source LLC
Chambersburg PA
CBHW020900160426
43192CB00007B/1012